Love's Final Solution

Love's Final Solution

Rev. F.E. Vorrath

Essence
PUBLISHING

Belleville, Ontario, Canada

Love's Final Solution

Copyright © 1998, Rev. F.E. Vorrath

All Scripture quotations, unless otherwise specified, are from the *King James Version* of the Bible.

ISBN: 1-896400-98-1

Essence Publishing is a Christian Book Publisher dedicated to furthering the work of Christ through the written word. For more information, contact: 44 Moira Street West, Belleville, Ontario, Canada K8P 1S3. Phone: 1-800-238-6376. Fax: (613) 962-3055.
Email: info@essence.on.ca
Internet: www.essence.on.ca

Printed in Canada
by

Essence
PUBLISHING

Acknowledgement

Grateful appreciation is extended
to my dear wife, Freda,
who has been very patient with my absence
during the preparation of this book.

Table of Contents

Preface

While this book is designed for personal edification, it is also useful for group study.

It is also a guide to the cardinal doctrines of the Christian Church.

I have taken a new approach to the Book of Revelation. I have approached it with the idea of God's love for man in the creation of man; in sustaining man through the ages; in God's provision of salvation and in His intimate fellowship in the present time period and for the future. The book of Revelation is God's Final Solution for the redemption of mankind.

Foreword

BY REV. J.B. KELLER

As we approach the year 2000 there is a growing interest in predictions of the future. Predicting the future has become a growth industry. However, those who rely upon ouija boards, tarot cards or even channeling spirits discover that these prophecies have a very high failure rate.

Peter tells us that "we also have a more sure word of prophecy; whereunto ye do well that ye take heed...." God's prophets had to have a one hundred percent accuracy rate, or they were discredited. Yet, even expository writers of Biblical prophecy have erred. Some have been carried away in their enthusiasm and have set dates for Christ's return only to find Christ did not show up at the anticipated time. Others did not pay the price of scholarship, of comparing Scripture with Scripture. In the day of instant coffee, instant pudding and gratification, there is a tendency to look for instant answers in the study of God's Word. A decade or two later, events prove them wrong.

You will find that Brother Vorrath's exposition of the Book of Revelation is a very careful treatment of the prophecy of "last things" that come from years of careful study and research. Rev. Vorrath began the Christian ministry in 1940 and pastored very faithfully until 1979. Though retired from active ministry, he has continued to study the Holy Scriptures, and especially prophecy. His book, *Love's Final Solution*, is the culmination of a lifetime of study of what the Holy Scriptures teach about end-time prophecy.

You will find that his views are formed by comparing Scripture with Scripture, for "no prophecy of Scripture is of any private interpretation." He does not support his views by quoting big names or well-known authors, but by reference to other Scriptures. His teaching comes directly from the Word of God. This is indeed refreshing.

The title of his exposition is particularly appropriate – Love's Final Solution. Christ will deal in love as He brings the plan of redemption to its culmination. Christ in love reveals what will be the final rewards and ultimate positions of the three groups of saints, the Church of Jesus Christ, the Old Testament Saints and the Tribulation Saints. He makes a very clear distinction between the Church, the Bride of Christ and the Jewish nation, the Wife of God the Father. It is also in love that Christ reveals what will be the future of God's chosen earthly nation, the descendants of Abraham. Finally, Christ must also deal with those who persistently reject him. There too, Love has a Final Solution.

Rev. Vorrath has also set out to elaborate on the major doctrines of Christian teaching as they come into view in the Book of Revelation. He expands on the teachings, for example, of the Rapture, when Christ comes for His Bride, the Judgment Seat of Christ, the Marriage Supper, the Return of Christ to set His Millennial Kingdom, and others.

It has been the good fortune of my wife and myself to have known Rev. Vorrath for 45 years. It has also been our privilege to be in his Sunday School class when he took us through the Book of Revelation, verse by verse, over a six month period. I have not heard better teaching on prophecy.

I recommend this major work to you, without reservation, for personal reading and edification, for personal in-depth study, and for group study. As you consider *Love's Final Solution*, together with a copy of the Bible before you, you will have an enriching experience.

Rev. J.B. Keller, B.A., B.Ed., P.G. Dip.
Retired pastor and teacher
President of Hillcrest Christian College, 1954-59
Surrey, British Columbia

Foreword

BY DR. JOHN A. KAISER

Over the span of 50 years, the author's life has touched mine at significant times and in meaningful ways. Rev. Fred Vorrath was our pastor when I was a teenager and he consistently modeled the Christian Spirit and pastoral leadership. I have good memories of the confirmation class he taught at our country church in southern Alberta, and he was one of the officiating ministers at our wedding. We served as colleagues in the same denominational fellowship for 24 years. At the time of this writing, I am honoured to serve as interim pastor of Fred and Freda's home church in Richmond, BC.

From personal visits and reading of this manuscript, I note the same thorough scholarship and careful attention to detail that I remember from those catechetical lessons 50 years ago.

His deep love for the Lord and His Word, his sincere interest in people, his rich sense of humour and enthusiasm for life make his writing interesting and rewarding to read. His analytical insight and vivid illustrations make difficult passages come alive and understandable.

Love's Final Solution is a significant contribution to the understanding of God's revealed will concerning the very important "end times."

Dr. John A. Kaiser

Introduction

The Expression of Love

Paul, the apostle, in writing to the Corinthian church, described the way and dealings of love as "the most excellent way." In 1 Corinthians 13:8, Paul emphasizes the fact that "love never fails."

The Breath of Life

In Genesis 1:27 we read, "So God created man in His own image," and again in Genesis 2:7, we read, "And the Lord God formed man from the dust of the ground and breathed into his nostrils the breath of life, and man became a living soul" (NIV). It would certainly by true to say that the "breath of life" included the "fruit of the spirit" and one of the fruits is love (Gal. 5:22). And it is a love that is reciprocal between God and man. The Scriptures are, from first to last, shot through with this truth. And it is reasonable enough to speak of God's creative act as eternal. In Christ, the Father God has revealed His love in a personal way for His creature man. By God's special act man becomes a living soul. And here is reference to breath of life, which man shares with the animal world; yet with this distinction, that "God Himself breathed into man's nostrils the breath of life" which was not the case with the animals.

A Great Difference

Genesis 1:20 and 24 say: "And God said, Let the waters bring forth abundantly the moving creature that hath life, and fowl that may fly above the earth in open firmament of heaven. And God said, Let the earth bring forth the living creature after his kind, cattle, and creeping thing, and beast of the earth after his kind, and it was so." But in the case of man, Genesis 2:7 says: "And the Lord God formed man of the dust of the ground, and breathed into his nostrils the breath of life; and man became a living soul." In this distinction it becomes clear that man was made in the "image" and after the "likeness" of God. And in this regard, God shows His love and concern for man (Gen. 1:26).

God's Remnant

And so through the various dispensations, God had compassion on a remnant of His creatures who practice allegiance to Him. To the serpent God said: "It (the woman's seed) shall bruise thy head, and thou shalt bruise his heel" (Gen. 3:15). There was to be enmity between the seed of the woman and the serpent. In His love for man, God foresaw His Son, Christ Jesus, crushing the power of Satan and procuring salvation for man. In like manner, Noah found favour in the eyes of the Lord and was saved through the flood that destroyed the corrupt people of his time. Genesis 6 speaks of the wickedness of man and how God would destroy them by a flood but "Noah found grace in the eyes of the Lord" (Gen. 6:8). And what can we say of the love God bestowed on Jacob, David, Samuel, the prophets and the people of the time of Daniel? Among the rebellious people, God always saved a remnant who practiced allegiance to Him. To Elijah God said: "Yet I have left me seven thousand in Israel, all the knees which have not bowed unto Baal" (1 Kings 19:18).

The Word Incarnate

In the New Testament, too, "God so loved the world that He gave His only begotten Son, that whosoever believeth in Him should not perish but have everlasting life" (John 3:16). Because of God's love for man, "The word became flesh and lived for a while among us," to reveal to us the glory of Himself and His Father (John 1:14). And such reciprocal love, as exists between husband and wife, must exist also between Christ and His Church (Eph. 5:32). God, through Christ, will not be denied. His love for His own will conquer and overcome every obstacle. In all the dispensations – Innocency, Conscience, Human Government, Promise, Law, Grace and Kingdom – God revealed His love for man in order to save man from sin and make him a worthy member of His Church and eternal destiny.

Why?

But before we deal with man's eternal destiny, we must ask ourselves the question, "Why is God so interested in man – His creation?"

The events outlined in Luke 16:19-31 are well known.

Remember

"There was a certain rich man, which was clothed in purple and fine linen, and fared sumptuously every day: And there was a certain beggar named Lazarus, which was laid at his gate, full of sores, and desiring to be fed with crumbs which fell from the rich man's table: moreover the dogs came and licked his sores.

"And it came to pass, that the beggar died, and was carried by the angels into Abraham's bosom; the rich man also died and was buried: And in hell he lift up his eyes, being in torments, and seeth Abraham afar off, and Lazarus in his bosom. And he cried and said, Father Abraham, have mercy on me, and send Lazarus, that he may dip the tip of his finger in water, and cool my tongue; for I am tormented in this flame.

"But Abraham said, Son remember that thou in thy lifetime receivedst thy good things, and likewise Lazarus evil things: but now he is comforted, and thou art tormented. And besides all this, between us and you there is a great gulf fixed: so that they which would pass from hence to you cannot; neither can they pass to us, that would come from thence.

"Then he said, I pray thee, therefore, father, that thou wouldest send him to my father's house: For I have five brethren; that he may testify unto them, lest they also come into this place of torment. Abraham saith unto him, they have Moses and the prophets; let them hear them.

"And he said, Nay, father Abraham: but if one went unto them from the dead, they will repent. And he said unto him, if they hear not Moses and the *prophets, neither will they be persuaded, though one rose from the dead."*

Here we see that after death the rich man found himself in hell and in torment while Lazarus found himself at Abraham's side and comforted. Their bodies were buried but their souls were aware of reality.

THE TRINITY OF MAN

Dissection

In order to study the trinity of man, in whom God shows such great interest, let us dissect the human being and discover what he is made of. The psalmist has the right idea when he says: "For I am fearfully and wonderfully made" (Ps. 139:14). That man is more than dust after the touch of God upon him, and that man is a triunity or a being consisting of three parts, is not an invention of man, but of God. It differentiates man from the animals and nullifies evolution. In 1 Thessalonians 5:23 we read: "And the very God of peace sanctify you wholly; and I pray God your whole spirit and soul and body be preserved blameless unto the coming of our Lord Jesus Christ."

The Same Idea

The same idea is expressed in Hebrews 4:12: "For the word of God is quick, and powerful, and sharper than any two-edged sword, piercing even to the dividing asunder of soul and spirit, and of the joints and marrow, and is a discerner of the thoughts and intents of the heart."

This trinity or triunity of body, soul and spirit, we find in a number of other systems. Let us name three:

Space

A. Space can be divided into only three dimensions... length, breadth and height. No thinker can plan a structure of more dimensions.

Matter

B. Matter fills space... and can be divided into energy, motion and phenomena (a thing as it appears to us) such as light, air and sound.

Time

C. Time can be divided only into past, present and future.

So the three, space, matter and time, all can be divided into three again. But why three? Because God so planned it.

The Trinity

God also is a trinity... Father, Son and Holy Spirit. God so loved mankind, made in the image and likeness of God, as to send His Son, to save mankind; and He sent His Holy Spirit to save, to guide, to comfort and dwell within mankind.

Man a Trinity

Man, too, is a trinity... body, soul and spirit. In this respect, man is made in the image of God, also a trinity.

A Difference

That the soul and spirit are not the same is proven by the fact that they can be separated. In this regard read again Hebrews 4:12; 1 Thessalonians 5:23; Micah 6:7; 1 Corinthians 15:44.

Micah 6:7b... "shall I give my firstborn for my transgression, the fruit of my body for the sin of my soul?"

1 Corinthians 15:44... "It is sown a natural body; it is raised a spiritual body. There is a natural body, and there is a spiritual body."

The Body

Let us consider first the body of a human being. We can see the body and can feel and touch it. It is called *guwphah* in the Old Testament and *soma* in the Greek New Testament. Through the body the soul expresses itself. Take for example sight. The eye is a marvellous directional instrument. The rumbling of the earbones give expression to words that can be heard. Then consider the importance of taste and touch. When in pain we shed tears and who can explain tears? If hurt, we mourn and how well can anyone explain the act of mourning? And we are, as yet, trying to discover the exact functions of glands – the pituitary gland is situated in the head and secretes five different hormones, one of which controls growth. The pineal gland has not really been analyzed. The thyroid gland can cause nervousness. The thymus gland, the adrenal gland, and the pancreas and gonad glands need also be mentioned. With the body we are world-conscious; we can touch, smell, see, hear and taste, as well as walk and talk. Christ was like us in His mortal body but without sin. And Paul says to the Corinthian church, "For ye are bought with a price; therefore glorify God in your body, and in your spirit, which are God's."

The Body and Soul

The body is not the soul. In 1 Kings 17:21-22 we read: "And he (Elijah) stretched himself upon the child three times, and cried unto the Lord, and said, O Lord my God, I pray thee, let this child's soul come into him again. And the Lord heard the voice of Elijah; and the soul of the child came into him again, and he revived." And in Matthew 10:28 we read: "And fear not them which kill the body, but are not able to kill the soul: but rather fear him which is able to destroy both soul and body in hell." In Revelation 6:9-10 we have further proof that the body is not the soul. Here the souls under the altar, whose bodies were slain on earth, cried unto God to avenge their blood on them that lived on earth. Let us read Scripture. "And when he had opened the fifth seal, I saw under the altar the souls of them that were slain for the word of God, and for the testimony which they held; and they cried with a loud voice, saying, how long, O Lord, holy and true, dost thou not judge and avenge our blood on them that dwell on the earth?"

The Soul

In connection with the soul having the capacity to be self in man, we become aware of man's brain. Better than any computer, it has been described as "a silent-running dynamo of memory and reason that makes every computer toylike by comparison" (by Gary Turbak in Kiwanis magazine of the brain, June/July 1991). The brain is the most highly organized and complicated entity in the world. Deep within the brain is the control center that controls organ operation, digestion and temperature control. It holds billions of times more data than even the most powerful computer. Just think about all the memories you have filed away from childhood and teen years and older years. And scores of friendships, faces, dates, historical data and how-to knowledge.

The soul, in the Old Testament, is called *nephesh,* and in the New Testament *psuche.* It is the self in a person, and causes us to be self-conscious in our will, imagination, conscience, memory, reason and affections. Jesus said: "My soul is exceeding sorrowful" (Matthew 26:38); and in Matthew 11:29 He says: "and ye shall find rest unto your souls;" meaning, not rest for the body, but rest for anxiety and desires and emotions. When in John 12:27 He says: "now is my soul troubled," He speaks not of the body but of "self." And God says: "And thou shalt love the Lord thy God with all thy soul." He refers not to the body, but to the affections. God loves the whole man, just as He made him, and that truth has reference to the title of this book.

The Spirit

In His love and concern for man, God also implanted a spirit within us so that he could have fellowship with mankind. Especially with those who are His. In Romans 8:16 we read: "The Spirit itself beareth witness with our spirit, that we are the children of God."

The Old Testament word for spirit is *ruwach* meaning air, breath or wind (Gen. 1:2; 2:7) where it says: "And the spirit of God moved upon the face of the waters." "And the Lord God formed man of the dust of the ground, and breathed into his nostrils the breath of life; and man became a living soul."

The New Testament word is *pneuma*. In John 3:8 and Acts 2:2 the Spirit is portrayed and compared to wind. "The wind bloweth where it listeth, and thou hearest the sound thereof, but canst not tell whence it cometh, and whither it goeth: so is every one that is born of the spirit." "And suddenly there came a sound from heaven as of a rushing mighty wind, and it filled all the house where they were sitting."

A Living Being

When God formed man from the dust of the ground and breathed into his nostrils the breath of life, man became a living soul or being. The dust had now received a soul to feel and a spirit to know right from wrong. 1 Corinthians 2:11 says: "for what man knoweth the things of man, save the spirit of man which is in him... even so the things of God knoweth no man but the Spirit of God." So that through our spirit we become God-conscious.

The spirit of man has to do with faith, hope, reverence, prayer and worship. In prayer, the body may sit, stand or kneel; the soul feels sorry, sad, joyous or contrite; and the spirit may hope, believe or reverence (worship God).

The Whole Person

In James 2:26, the writer explains that "the body without the spirit is dead." And we conclude that the body, upon death, goes to the grave, but the soul and spirit are those which are "absent from the body and are present with the Lord" (2 Cor. 5:8). And Paul in Philippians 1:23 adds: "...having a desire to depart, and to be with Christ." Then, in the resurrection of the body (in the rapture or even in the final resurrection) the whole person shall stand before God. It shall be the whole person in a spiritual body. 1 Thessalonians 5:23 says: "And the very God of peace sanctify you wholly; and I pray God your whole spirit and soul and body be preserved blameless unto the coming of our Lord Jesus Christ."

Prepared

God's love reaches out to the spirit-filled Christian, serving the Lord acceptably until He comes to take us to be with Him. A look at Revelation, as it was given to John, will help us to prepare ourselves even now for His soon coming.

Love's Reaches

And now we come to the Revelation and Love's Final Solution. The love of God, as revealed in Jesus Christ His Son, will reveal how, once more, God, through Jesus Christ, will try to woo mankind to accept and follow Him. There must not be any excuse for being in the dark about the facts of Revelation. We need not fear the judgments of God since we belong to Him in that we have committed ourselves to Him. We must not belong to those in Psalm 2 of whom it is written: "The heathen rage. The people imagine a vain thing. The kings and rulers take counsel against the Lord, and against his anointed. Saying, Let us break their bands asunder, and cast their cords from us." These do not like His way and will be sharing in the judgments of God. For even judgments and punishment can be a token of divine love. God's dealing with sin will certainly show God's mercy as far as ever it can reach. Hebrews 12:6 reveals this truth. It says: "For whom the Lord loveth He chasteneth and scourgeth every son whom He receiveth." And in His call for repentance He says in Revelation 3:19: "As many as I love, I rebuke and chasten." Because of the soul's survival after death, God allows tribulation as a means to save any who will allow themselves to be saved. Why else does Peter, in 1 Peter 3:19-20 say that "Christ also went and preached unto the spirits in prison; who sometime were disobedient when the longsuffering of God waited in the days of Noah"? The supreme penalty for sin is unquestionably the loss of God's love and Kingdom.

Various Punishments

Regarding punishment, man has invented many ways of doing away with fellowmen. We may enumerate some: stoning, hanging, burning, torture, suffocation, exposure, flogging, imprisonment, mutilation and slavery. Even chemicals have been used. In some cases, bitter anger and revenge were the cause of such punishment. But according to the Word of God, hell was prepared for the devil and his followers. Not out of revenge but because of disobedience and rebellion. Luke, in Luke 19:10, says: "For the son of man is come to seek and to save that which was lost." For God so loved, that He gave His only begotten son. And that divine love carries right through the Revelation given to John. And it is the last call to man when in Revelation 22:17 the cry goes out: "And the spirit and the bride say, come. And let him that heareth say, come. And let him that is athirst come."

God's Final Call

It is, therefore, the triune God who extends this invitation in these latter days. Hebrews 1:1-2 says: "God, who at sundry times and in divers manners spake in times past unto the fathers by the prophets. Hath in these last days spoken unto us by His Son." His Son, as the Gift of love, declares "Love's Final Solution" for mankind in the Revelation given to the apostle John.

The Revelation of Jesus Christ Given to John

Being Aware of God's Presence

In Matthew 16:28 Jesus said: "There be some who are standing here will not taste death before they see the Son of Man coming in his kingdom." John and other disciples were given the opportunity to see that kingdom on the Mount of Transfiguration and now in receiving the revelation. Chapter 4:8 gives us the order: "Holy, holy, holy, Lord God Almighty, which was, and is, and is to come." And chapter 1:8 says: "I am Alpha and Omega, the beginning and the ending, saith the Lord, which is, and which was, and which is to come, the Almighty." Here we understand three time periods:

Time Periods

1. What you have seen – Jesus the revelator and Jesus risen.
2. What is now – the church age.
3. What will take place later – after the church age – the tribulation and judgment and eternity.

Along with the foregoing division, we must say that the revelation deals with three groups of people; the Church, the nation of Israel and the Gentile nations.

What You Have Seen

The Book is called the *Apokalupsis* or, in the English language, the Apocalypse. The word denotes "disclosure," as in removal of a veil. It implies the lifting up of a curtain, so all can see what is uncovered; as at Jesus' death "the veil of the temple was rent in the midst." In script or writing, it means "a making clear," and if applied to a person, it denotes "visible presence." To John it would mean a revealing of Jesus Himself and what He is about to do. But the expression "the revelation of Jesus Christ" need not mean one concerning Christ, rather *from* Him.

A Mysterious Way

God gave Jesus this revelation. And this revelation was given by Jesus to an angel who in turn gave it to John, the servant of Christ. The message was not to be hidden but revealed. Daniel was to seal the book to the time of the end (Dan. 12:4). But here the message was to be proclaimed. The word for servant is *doulos* and denoted slave or bondservant, one intimately tied in with Jesus. And so the love of God moves in a mysterious way, His wonders to perform.

God's Time Table

When Jesus speaks of "things which must shortly come to pass," we must not infer that these events will come to pass today or tomorrow, but we must take note of how God counts time. Peter speaks of this in 2 Peter 3:8 when he says: "But, beloved, be not ignorant of this one thing, that one day is with the Lord as a thousand years, and a thousand years as one day." And remember that these "last days" of Hebrews 1:2 have already continued for almost two thousand years. God counts time differently than man does.

John faithfully proclaimed the message of revelation to the churches as to two outstanding facts. One, as the Word of God, which implies authority. And then John proclaims it as the testimony of Jesus Christ. It rings so true what Jesus said in Mark 13:31, when He said: "Heaven and earth shall pass away; but my words shall not pass away." We must remind ourselves that only God knows the time of all that shall transpire, but according to Revelation 22:10, we are to hear it. And so, "Blessed is he that readeth and heareth and keepeth the words of this prophecy." And John saw prophecy fulfilled. "The time is at hand." These words show certainty. It will happen. The signs of His coming are being fulfilled. Jesus said there should come "false christs" who would deceive many (Matt. 24). To name only one such: Father Divine of Detroit, Michigan, claimed to be Christ and married a woman and called her the bride of Christ and claimed fifty thousand adherents. There are also false prophets and we notice them in various cults. There shall also be wars and rumors of war. War, in this world of ours, has not ceased. The fires of rebellion are ever present. Countries have been experiencing poverty and starvation, but have seemingly enough finances to purchase war materials. Jesus said there would be famines. Right here we ought to examine our eating habits. When two couples can go out for dinner and leave one hundred and fifty dollars for their meal, one wonders just what they consumed. There shall be earthquakes and plagues. They are too numerous to mention. Of plagues we can mention at least two – cancer and AIDS.

Trends

Trends, too, play an important role in our day. I walked into a business place one day and there stood a boy with the imprint on each trouser leg, namely, "rebel." Close relatives and friends are being killed for their possessions. Hair styles and clothes are way out. There are churches of Satan and high priests of Satan. Young people are committing suicide. Wealth, too, is a sign of the times. It allows for excesses. In Revelation 17 and 18, the kings of the earth shall mourn for lost wealth. Love shall wax cold, even in Christians. Marriage and family ties are broken.

A Vision?

Just how the angel communicated the message, we do not know. Perhaps in a vision. Verse ten in chapter one says: "I was in the spirit... and heard behind me a great voice, as of a trumpet. Let us be satisfied with that summation.

Human Instrumentality

Verse four describes John as the writer to the seven churches. God has other methods of bringing the message to the attention of the churches, but He uses human vessels, since they are capable of human love and compassion. The seven churches indicate representative assemblies. They represent all of the churches of the time period and include, no doubt, all of church history. The church is to remain under grace (unmerited favour) and peace (heart peace which is unchangeable). Such grace and peace is Christ given and steadies the child of God. And it comes from the Eternal One... who was, is and is to come.

The Seven Spirits

The seven Spirits are the "fullness" of one Spirit. In Isaiah 11:1-2 we have the Spirit in His offices: First, His deity; second, of wisdom; third, of understanding; fourth, of counsel; fifth, of might; sixth, of knowledge; and seventh, of the fear of Jehovah.

Christ

Then we see Jesus Christ, the faithful witness. Paul says to Timothy (1 Tim. 6:13) of Jesus that He "before Pilate witnessed a good confession." And John (John 7:7) states that the world hates Jesus "because I testify of it, that the works thereof are evil." Jesus is qualified to do so because He is the "firstborn" of the dead. The word used is *prototokos*, the first of the dead, who was raised to eternal life. Others were raised to die again. He is raised and lives eternally and has become the head of all creation. He is the "ruler" of the kings of the earth. The question here is, who shall rule? Satan and mankind or God by Christ Jesus?

Without a doubt, God by Christ. The word "loved," in verse five, is in the present tense. The word "loosed" (washed) is in the past tense. The loosing was done once. The loving goes on forever. It agrees with the title "Love's Final Solution." Once more, in these latter days – even during terrible tribulation – the call goes forth. God loves those who will submit to Him and follow His will.

A Kingdom

In verse six the original language has it as "and has made us a kingdom and priests unto God." We need to compare this expression with the words of chapter 5:10, "and madest them... unto our God a kingdom and priests and they will reign on the earth." We are already designated "kings and priests" but do not reign as yet. As yet our God has power (might) and authority that never cease.

A Foreview

In verse seven John is given a public revelation of Jesus. All shall see him. It is a foreview of Revelation 20, when He shall come visibly to judge the wicked. It has no bearing on the "dead in Christ" who with the "living in Christ" will be seized into the clouds and meet the Lord in the air, as it is related in 1 Thessalonians 4.

A Mourning

Those who pierced Him shall mourn. This is what the prophet Zechariah had in mind when he writes about the mourning of Israel in chapter 12:10-11. Here is what he says: "And I will pour upon the house of David, and upon the inhabitants of Jerusalem, the spirit of grace and of supplications: and they shall look upon me whom they have pierced, and they shall mourn for him, as one that is in bitterness for his firstborn. In that day shall there be a great mourning in Jerusalem." Then verse eight of Revelation shows the Lord being all in all. He is the Beginning and the End. Here on earth judgment is entrusted to the Holy Spirit whom God sent upon Christ's ascension: John 14:16-17 says: "And I will pray the Father, and He shall give you another comforter, that He may abide with you forever; even the Spirit of truth." In heaven Jesus is known as the "Lamb slain." And finally, Christ is known as "Lord of lords and King of kings."

John the Beloved Disciple

The words "I John" in verse nine are a mark of being known. He was the beloved disciple and Peter asked the Lord what should transpire in his life after the Lord's ascension. The Lord said: "If I will that he tarry till I come, what is that to thee?" And now John is given a vision of Christ's kingdom age and love's final solution. The designation "brother" (*adelphos*) can lead the reader to a reference of the expression of "Philadelphia," the church of brotherly love (vs. 9). The word "companion" (Greek: co-sharer) proved that John writes not as exercising authority but as a "seer" unfolding the future in a humble and loving attitude.

Trouble

John speaks of tribulation first. The word is *thlipsis* in Greek, *tribulum* in the Latin. In the

Greek the word means "trouble" and in the Latin "threshing flail," separating the chaff from the wheat. Then John speaks of the kingdom assured to the children of God. And after this he speaks of the patience to wait for its manifestation. The people of God and His Christ suffer under those who in the last days say: "Where is the promise of His coming? For since the fathers fell asleep, all things continue as they were from the beginning of creation" (2 Pet. 3:4). And in 2 Thessalonians 1:4-5 we read: "So that we ourselves glory in you in the churches of God for your patience and faith in all your persecutions and tribulations that ye endure. Which is a manifest token of the righteous judgment of God that ye may be counted worthy of the kingdom of God, for which ye also suffer." This is the ordinary suffering of John which comes to God's children because of the hatred of the world. The world hates Christ and His followers. This speaks not of the great tribulation to follow. It speaks to each one of us who undergoes trials that come our way because we follow Christ.

Suffering

John was banished to the island of Patmos, a rocky, barren island in the Aegean Sea, during the reign of Domitian about A.D. 81-86 (A.D. meaning Anno Domini – in the year of the Lord). John suffered for his testimony of Christ. It is still possible to suffer for Christ in our day. Any open testimony is is resented by the world. And the time may be at hand when our testimony against immorality may be contested and prohibited by some who are in favour of those who practice such permissiveness.

The Lord's Day

The term "the Lord's Day," in verse ten, refers to what we consider our Sunday, the first day of the week. In Acts 20:7 we read: "And upon the first day of the week, when the disciples came together to break bread, Paul preached unto them, ready to depart on the morrow; and continued his speech until midnight." And in 1 Corinthians 16:2 again: "Upon the first day of the week let everyone of you lay by him in store, as God hath prospered him, that there be no gatherings when I come." It is the resurrection day and we believe that the followers of Jesus observed the Sunday, just as the Sabbath was given to be observed by the Jews. In Exodus 31:16-17 we read: Wherefore the children of Israel shall keep the Sabbath, to observe the Sabbath throughout their generations, for a perpetual covenant. It is a sign between me and the children of Israel forever."

The Lord's Day is not the "Day of the Lord" when Jesus deals with the ungodly world in wrath. It is too early for that great and terrible day in this part of the revelation. The church age is first of all addressed before that notable day of the Lord.

Week Days

Here we must consider the origin of week days. There were four influences that were brought together in Alexandria not very long before the Christian era to order the week. The conception of the influence of the planets was Babylonian. The mathematical working out of the order of the planets was Greek. The division of the day into twenty-four hours was Egyptian and the free continuous seven-day week was Jewish. The early Romans did not have a week at all but later they adopted the seven-day week and named it after the sun, moon and five other planets they knew about. Here they are:

Sun	–	Sunday (sun's day)
Moon	–	Monday (moon's day)
Tiv	–	Tuesday (war god)
Woden	–	Wednesday (chief of the gods)
Thunor	–	Thursday (thunder god)
Frig	–	Friday (goddess of marriage and wife of Woden)
Saturn's day	–	Saturday

So the days carry pagan names but God counted otherwise. He rested on the seventh day, the Sabbath, and our Lord arose on the first day, which must have been in use during the time of Christ on earth. In the expression of "Day of Creation," the word "day" is used of the whole period of creation, and with God a day can mean a thousand years. The word "day" can be used figuratively:

1. The span of human life – Gen. 5:4

2. An indefinite time – Gen. 3:14

3. A set time – Gen. 25:24

4. An historic period – Gen. 6:4

5. Past time – Ps. 18:18

6. Future time – Deut. 31:14

7. The eternal – Dan. 7:9,13 (God is called the Ancient of days)

8. A season of opportunity – John 9:4

9. A time of salvation – Rom. 13:12

In all of the foregoing we are dealing with the "things which thou hast seen," as recorded in verse nineteen.

Various Days

Next we must distinguish between the various "days" of Scripture. We may name them: "The Lord's Day," "The Day of Christ," "The Day of the Lord," and "The Day of God." Let us give a brief description of these days.

The Lord's Day

1. The Lord's Day. This is our Sunday. It is too early in Revelation for the terrible wrath of God to be revealed. John came to be in the Spirit on the Sunday (the Lord's Day).

The Day of Christ

2. The Day of Christ. This day we call the "blessed hope," for during this time the dead in Christ shall be raised and the living in Christ shall together be "seized" in the clouds to meet the Lord in the air and be with Him. What a comfort that will be. Here are some guiding Scriptures: 1 Corinthians 1:8, "Who shall also confirm you unto the end, that ye may be blameless in the day of our Lord Jesus Christ"; Philippians 1:10, "That ye may approve things that are excellent; that ye may be sincere and without offence till the day of

Christ"; 1 Corinthians 15:51-52, "Behold, I show you a mystery: We shall not all sleep, but we shall all be changed. In a moment, in the twinkling of an eye, at the last trump: for the trumpet shall sound, and the dead shall be raised incorruptible, and we shall be changed"; 1 Thessalonians 4:16-17. "For the Lord himself shall descend from heaven with a shout, with the voice of the archangel, and with the trump of God: and the dead in Christ shall rise first: Then we which are alive and remain shall be caught up together with them in the clouds, to meet the Lord in the air: and so shall we ever be with the Lord."

Only those who are changed without dying are able to say: "O death, where is thy sting? O grave, where is thy victory?" Titus 2:13 also is comforting to the Christian. "Looking for that blessed hope, and the glorious appearing of the great God and our Saviour Jesus Christ."

The Seizure

The rapture or seizure of the church will be for many a surprise. Matthew 24:42 is a marching order for all believers. It says: "Watch, therefore: for ye know not what hour your Lord doth come." The trump of God that Paul mentions is not the trumpet of an angel. In Numbers 10:2 we read: "Make thee two trumpets of silver; of a whole piece shalt thou make them: that thou mayest use them for the calling of the assembly, and for the journeying of the camps." The first trumpet was for getting ready for travel. The last trumpet call was for travelling. It is this trumpet call that concerns the church. If the church is to go through the tribulation, as some maintain, then instead of waiting for the Lord, we should be waiting for the tribulation.

In Daniel 9:27 we read: "And he shall confirm the covenant with many for one week: and in the midst of the week he shall cause the sacrifice and the oblation to cease, and for the over-spreading of abominations he shall make it desolate, even until the consumption, and that determined shall be poured upon the desolate." The prince (beast-antichrist) shall come at the *beginning* of the week (last seven years) but before that comes to pass, the "He" of 2 Thessalonians 2:7-8a must be taken away. "For the mystery of iniquity doth already work: only 'He' who now letteth will let, until 'He' be taken out of the way." "And then shall that wicked be revealed." In the Greek, the word "He" is a personal pronoun, in the masculine gender, and must refer to a person. We believe He is the Holy Spirit and lives within the Church (Christians), and when removed, will include all born-again children of God.

Jacob's Trouble

In dealing with the rapture, we must also say that the tribulation is *not* the perfecting of the saints. The church has nothing to do with the tribulation. It is the time of "Jacob's Trouble" as shown in Jeremiah 30:7 where we read: "Alas! for that day is great, so that none is like it: it is even the time of Jacob's trouble, but he shall be saved out of it." It is the judgment upon Israel. The church is not mentioned in it. Revelation 3:10 says: "Because thou has kept the word of my patience, I also will keep thee from the hour of temptation, which shall come upon all the world, to try them that dwell upon the earth." And in 1 Thessalonians 1:10 we read: "And to wait for his Son from heaven, whom he raised from the dead, even Jesus, which delivered us *from* the *wrath to come.*" And 1 Thessalonians 5:9 says: "For God hath not appointed us to wrath, but to obtain salvation by our Lord Jesus Christ."

Confusion

The confusion about the rapture comes from and is due to failing to distinguish between Christ's coming 'for' His saints and 'with' His saints. Such Scriptures as will be quoted will clarify the matter. Zechariah 14:5b: "And ye shall flee to the valley of the mountains and the Lord my God shall come, and all the saints with thee." Colossians 3:4: "When Christ, who is our life, shall appear, then shall ye also appear with him in glory." 1 Thessalonians 3:13: "To the end he may stablish your hearts unblameable in holiness before God, even our Father, at the coming of our Lord Jesus Christ with all his saints." Jude 14: "And Enoch also, the seventh from Adam, prophesied of these, saying, Behold, the Lord cometh with ten thousands of his saints."

The Judgment Seat of Christ

In line with what we have said about the rapture, we must make reference to the judgment seat of Christ. In 2 Corinthians 5:10 we read: "For we must all appear before the judgment seat of Christ; that every one may receive the things done in his body, according to that he has done, whether it be good or bad." Romans 14:10b: "For we shall all stand before the judgment seat of Christ." There are five different judgments spoken of in the Bible; actually seven if we differentiate somewhat – the judgment upon sin in the death of Christ. In Hebrews 2:17 we read: "Wherefore in all things it behoved him to be made like unto his brethren, that he might be a merciful and faithful high priest in things pertaining to God, to make reconciliation for the sins of the people." There is also the judgment of believers. They purify themselves. 1 Peter 4:17a says: "For the time is come that judgment must begin at the house of God." Then we have the judgment upon believer's works. 1 Corinthians 3:11-15 says: "For other foundation can no man lay than that is laid, which is Jesus Christ. Now if any man build upon this foundation gold, silver, precious stones, wood, hay, stubble; Every man's work shall be made manifest: for the day shall declare it because it shall be revealed by fire; and the fire shall try every man's work of what sort it is. If any man's work abide which he hath built thereupon, he shall receive a reward. If any man's work shall be burned, he shall suffer loss; but he himself shall be saved; yet so as by fire."

There is also the judgment of the Jews. Ezekiel 20:37 says: "And I will cause you to pass under the rod and I will bring you into the bond of the covenant." There is also the judgment upon the nations. Matthew 25:32 says: "And before Him shall be gathered all nations: and he shall separate them one from another, as a shepherd divideth his sheep from the goats." There will be the judgment upon the satanic powers. Jude 6 says: "And the angels which kept not their first estate, but left their own habitation, he has reserved in everlasting chains under darkness unto the judgment of the great day." Then there is the judgment of the wicked dead (the Great White Throne Judgment) (Rev. 20:11-15).

Crowns

And crowns are awarded to those Christians who are worthy to receive them. There is the *Incorruptible Crown* (Victor's crown). 1 Corinthians 9:25 reads: "And every man that striveth for the mastery is temperate in all things. Now they do it to obtain a corruptible crown; but we an incorruptible." The *Crown of Life* is the martyr's crown. Revelation 2:10b says: "Be thou faithful unto death, and I will give thee a crown of life." The *Crown of Glory* is the elder's crown. 1 Peter 5:4 says: "And when the chief Shepherd shall appear, ye shall receive a crown of glory that fadeth not away." The *Crown of Righteousness* is for those who love His appearing. 2 Timothy 4:8 reads: "Henceforth there is laid up for me a crown of righteousness, which the Lord, the righteous judge, shall give me at that day: and not to me only, but unto all them also that love his appearing." The *Crown of Rejoicing* is the soul-winner's crown. 1 Thessalonians 2:19 says: "For what is our hope, or joy, or crown of rejoicing? Are not even ye in the presence of our Lord Jesus Christ at his coming."

God's Wife

The church, as the Bride of Christ, is invited to the marriage supper. Revelation 19:7 says: "Let us be glad and rejoice, and give honour to him: for the marriage of the Lamb is come, and his wife hath made herself ready." Israel is God's wife. Hosea 2:19 says: "And I will betroth thee unto me for ever; ye, I will betroth thee onto me in righteousness, and in judgment, and in lovingkindness, and in mercies." And Israel is not the Church. The marriage falls likely between the translation of the saints and the second coming in glory. The place may be in heaven, as it is from the air that the Church comes when He returns. Revelation 19:14 says: "And the armies which were in heaven followed him upon white horses, clothed in fine linen, white and clean." There will, no doubt, be guests and friends at the supper (John the Baptist, John 3:29, was a friend of the bridegroom).

Some Reasons

We note some reasons why the Church will not be in the great tribulation. But let us first say that the Church is the body of Christ, the born-again people from Pentecost to Christ's Second Coming. 1 Corinthians 12:27 says: "Now ye are the body of Christ, and members in particular." And Ephesians 5:27 says: "That He might present it to himself a glorious church, not having spot, or wrinkle, or any such thing; but that it should be holy and without blemish." We do not mean by the "church" the religious profession.

Tribulation

We mean by the Great Tribulation that "time of trouble spoken by Daniel, Jeremiah and other prophets. Also spoken of by our Lord and the apostles. Mark 13:19 says: "For in those days shall be affliction, such as was not from the beginning of the creation which God created unto this time, neither shall be." Its duration is seven years. However, the wrath of God is of only three and a half years.

We know that most of the Church cannot go through the tribulation, for the vast majority of her, for nearly two thousand years, has already gone to be with Christ, to return with Him at His second coming. Why should a small number at the end be subjected to a test and trial? It is only from "divine wrath," not human, that we affirm the Church of God to be delivered. God has put the hope of translation into his saints so they can say "we will together be caught up in the clouds to meet the Lord in the air, in a moment, in the twinkling of an eye." This hope is their comfort.

The Sabbath

In Matthew 24, our Lord, after speaking of a great tribulation such as has not been, nor will be, He says: "Pray ye that your flight be not in winter, neither on the Sabbath." The Church has nothing to do with winter or Sabbath. It is for the Jewish people, God's earthly people. The constant use of such words as "look for His appearing," "wait for God's Son," "love His appearing," in the Epistles, shows how God keeps this hope alive in His people and children.

The great tribulation is not once mentioned by Paul in his epistles, Romans to Philemon, nor is it spoken of in Hebrews, nor are the saints warned of it. Perilous times are spoken of, but not the Great Tribulation.

The Seventieth Week

The seventieth week of Daniel, lasting seven years, has two halves, in neither of which the Church can be on earth. There is no other place the tribulation can come but in the seventieth week of Daniel 9:27. "And he shall confirm the covenant with many for one week: and in the midst of the week he shall cause the sacrifice and the oblation to cease, and for the overspreading of abominations he shall make it desolate even until the consummation, and that determined shall be poured upon the desolate." It is antichrist that will make an agreement with Israel for one week and then break it after three and a half years. Not with the Church, but with Israel, the people of Daniel. Revelation 11 shows the first half of the week, and the chapter is Jewish. The scene is Jerusalem in the last days. John is to measure the temple and altar. The court of the temple is for the nations who will tread it under foot for forty-two months. This refers to the last half of the seven years. The next verse (vs. 3) refers to the first half and says: "And I will give unto my two witnesses and they shall prophesy a thousand two hundred and threescore days, clothed in sackcloth" (3 1/2 years). In chapter thirteen the antichrist does his pleasure for the last three and a half years. This cannot happen until the two witnesses are out of the way.

Christ Among the Churches

So we say, first "The things which thou sawest" are a vision of Christ among the churches in Revelation 1. Second, "The things which are" are the letters to the seven churches – an outline of church history. And thirdly, "The things which shall come to pass after these things" is the rest of Revelation from chapter four onward. We should be waiting for the Day of Christ.

The Day of the Lord

Scriptures dealing with this subject are: Joel 2:1b, "For the day of the Lord cometh, for it is nigh at hand"; 2 Thessalonians 2:2, "That ye be not soon shaken in mind, or be troubled, neither by spirit, nor by word, nor by letter as from us, as that the day of the Lord is at hand" (day of Christ wrongly translated); Isaiah 13:9a, "Behold, the day of the Lord cometh, cruel both with wrath and fierce anger"; 2 Peter 3:10a, "But the day of the Lord will come as a thief in the night"; Acts 2:20, "The sun shall be turned into darkness, and the moon into blood, before that great and notable day of the Lord come."

The Sun of Righteousness

This is the second stage of Christ's second coming, known as the Revelation. It is Christ's visible coming as the "Sun of Righteousness," and being the Apocalypse. The incarnation hid His power, now His glory is seen. He comes to the Mount of Olives. Zechariah 14:4 says: "And his feet shall stand in that day upon the Mount of Olives, which is before Jerusalem on the east, and the Mount of Olives shall cleave in the midst thereof toward the east and toward the west, and there shall be a very great valley; and half of the mountain shall remove toward the north, and half of it toward the south."

Events

In the Day of the Lord certain events take place.

1. There shall be a Federation of states into the Roman Empire known as the Common Market (Daniel 2, 7). Here are mentioned the kingdoms of Babylon, Media Persia, Greece and Rome. These four kingdoms were represented by four beasts, the last of which had ten horns which represented ten kings. Another shall arise and pluck out three and he being the eighth. He shall think to change times and laws for three and a half years in dealing with the saints (Israel) (Dan. 7:25).

2. There comes the rise of the political ruler of this empire who makes a covenant with Israel (Dan. 9:27).

3. There will be a formation of a false religious system under the false prophet. Revelation 13:11-18: "And I behold another beast coming up out of the earth... And he doeth great wonders... and he causeth all, both small and great, rich and poor, free and bond, to receive a mark in their right hand, or in their foreheads... and his number is the number of a man."

4. There will be the pouring out of the judgments under the seals (Rev. 6).

5. There will be the separation of the 144,000 witnesses of Revelation 7.

6. There will be the trumpet judgments (Rev. 8-11).

7. There will be the rise of God's witnesses (Rev. 11).

8. Then see the persecution of Israel (Rev. 12).

9. Then come the pouring out of the bowls of judgment (Rev. 16).

10. There will be the overthrow of the false professing church (Rev. 17-18).

11. The events of Armageddon will take place (Ezek. 38-39; Rev. 16:16; 19:17-21).

12. Then the proclamation of the gospel of the Kingdom (Matt. 24:14).

13. The return of the Lord (Matt. 24).

14. The destruction of the Beast and False Prophet and followers (Rev. 19:11).

15. The judgment of the nations (Matt. 25:31-46).

16. The regathering of Israel (Ezek. 37:1-14).

17. The judgment of living Israel (Ezek. 20:33-38).

18. The restoration of Israel (Amos 9:15).

19. The binding of Satan (Rev. 20:2-3).

20. The millennial age and final revolt of Satan (Rev. 20:7-10).

21. The Great White Throne Judgment (Rev. 20:11-15).

22. The purging of the earth (new heaven and earth) (2 Pet. 3:10-13).

The Day of God

This is the day of the renovation of the earth by fire and it extends to eternity. 2 Peter 3:12 says:

"Looking for and hasting unto the coming of the day of God, wherein the heavens being on fire shall be dissolve, and the elements shall melt with fervent heat." And Revelation 21:1 says: "And I say a new heaven and a new earth: for the first heaven and the first earth were passed away."

Resurrections

In this connection, as regards the Day of Christ, we must mention also, if only briefly, concerning the various resurrections.

The first resurrection that needs mention is the resurrection of the "First Fruits." These are Christ and the saints. In Matthew 27:52-53 we read: "And the graves were opened; and many bodies of the saints which slept arose, and came out of the graves after his resurrection, and went into the holy city, and appeared unto many." Although the singular is used, it implies plurality. When it says in Ephesians 4:8: "Wherefore he saith, when he ascended upon high, he led captivity captive, and gave gifts unto men," we believe that he emptied the one compartment of hades or hell (known as Abraham's bosom) and took them to paradise, into which place Paul was caught up and heard unspeakable words (2 Cor. 12:4). Also to which place those saints in the Ephesus church received the promise to be (Rev. 2:7b). "To him that overcometh will I give to eat of the tree of life, which is in the midst of the paradise of God." There is here an interval of the present dispensation – the time of which is unknown.

We must also recognize the resurrection (so named) of the church-age saints known as the rapture. 1 Thessalonians 4:16-17 says: "For the Lord himself shall descend from heaven with a shout, with the voice of the archangel, and with the trumpet of God: and the dead in Christ shall rise first: then we which are alive and remain shall be caught up together with them in the clouds, to meet the Lord in the air: and so shall we ever be with the Lord." This is the harvest or ingathering. 1 Corinthians 15:51 says: "Behold, I show you a mystery; we shall not all sleep, but we shall all be changed."

Interval

Then there is another interval – the tribulation period of seven years duration. Here we may speak of the resurrection of the tribulation saints. Revelation 20:4 says: "And I saw thrones, and they sat upon them, and judgment was given unto them: and I saw the souls of them that were beheaded for the witness of Jesus, and for the word of God, and which had not worshiped the beast, neither his image, neither had received his mark upon their foreheads, or in their hands: and they lived and reigned with Christ a thousand years." It may be understood as occurring together with the Old Testament saints. Daniel 12:2 says: "And many of them that sleep in the dust of the earth shall awake, some to everlasting life, and some to shame and everlasting contempt." It occurs just before the second advent of Christ to earth. It is the glorious visible resurrection at Armageddon. All of those groups have their own time period.

A Final Resurrection

Then comes the final resurrection of the unsaved dead. Revelation 20:12 says: "And I saw the dead, small and great, stand before God; and the books were opened: and another book was opened, which is the book of life: and the dead were judged out of those things which were written in the books, according to their works." These are known as the tares of Matthew 13:28-30. And also known as the second resurrection and as the Great White Throne Judgment. It is at the end of the millennial age.

Theories of the Rapture

After our look at the resurrections, we must also consider some thoughts on the second coming of Christ. Christians hold to various positions:

1. The partial rapture theory. It claims that only those watching will be taken. It misunderstands the value of the death of Christ. The death frees the sinner from condemnation and makes him acceptable to God. It, therefore, denies the unity of the body of Christ.

2. The post-tribulation theory. It places the Church in the great tribulation which includes the wrath of God. It does not distinguish between Israel and the Church. It denies that the Lord may come at any time. 1 Corinthians 1:7 says: "So that ye come behind in no gift; waiting for the coming of our Lord Jesus Christ."

3. The mid-tribulation theory. It states that the Church will be raptured during the end of the first three and a half years of Daniel's seventieth week and at the sound of the trumpet of the seventh angel and at the catching up of the two witnesses in Revelation 11. Again, they deny the

distinction between Israel and the Church. If the Church goes into the first three and a half years, then the 144,000 would be saved into the Church. And they are different from the Church.

4. The pre-tribulation theory. It states and maintains that the entire Church body will be removed from the earth before any part of the seventieth week of Daniel begins.

In the Spirit

And now Revelation 1:10 is where John came to be "in the spirit." He had, no doubt, a vision as Daniel did. Daniel 2:19 says: "Then was the secret revealed unto Daniel in a night vision. Then Daniel blessed the God of heaven." Or as Zacharias did. Luke 1:22: "And when he came out, he could not speak unto them; and they perceived that he had seen a vision in the temple for he beckoned unto them and remained speechless." Or as Paul had in 2 Corinthians 12:1: "It is not expedient for me doubtless to glory. I will come to visions and revelations of the Lord." It would seem that a vision can be a dream, impression or visible image. The trumpet sound denotes authority. Christ is speaking like the sound of a trumpet and proves Himself as the First and the Last. John is to "write" and "send" the message to the seven churches. To Daniel it was said: "Seal the book to the time of the end" (Dan. 12:4).

The Voice

John, in verse twelve, turns to see the voice that spoke. Our Lord is the Word. Through Him

God speaks to us. Jesus gave us His Spirit to witness with our spirit that we are His children and can respond to Him. Romans 8:16 says: "The Spirit itself beareth witness with our spirit, that we are the children of God."

Lampstands

The golden candlesticks are "lampstands." A candlestick as Israel used had one straight and three out of each side, representing "Oneness." Here are seven. Each church is independently responsible to the Lord. The candlestick is not the light, but bears the light. The Church receives the light from Christ.

The Son of Man

Verse thirteen speaks of One like the Son of Man in the midst of the seven churches, clothed with "a garment down to the foot." It shows Him as High Priest and a Judge. Here is an eight-fold description of Christ. He is like the Son of Man. Such is His body. His hair is white as wool and snow. Daniel saw a similar figure. Daniel 7:9 says: "I beheld till the thrones were cast down, and the Ancient of days did sit, whose garment was white as snow, and the hair of his head like the pure wool." His eyes were as a flame of fire. His feet like fine brass. Daniel saw the same Person. Daniel 10:6b: "...and his face as the appearance of lightning, and his eyes as lamps of fire, and his arms and his feet like in colour to polished brass." His voice was like many waters. His right hand held the seven stars (messengers or pastors). His mouth had a two-edged sword coming out of it. Paul, in

Ephesians 6:17, says the sword of the spirit is the Word of God. His countenance was as the sun.

The Ancient of Days

The High Priest had to keep the candles burning. In our day pastors have a grave responsibility. In all of this description we behold that it is the "Ancient of Days" as depicted in Daniel 7:9-10,13,22 who holds sway over the overseers of the churches. His eyes are all-seeing and His Word is like a sword.

Absent from the Body

Regarding "death" in verse eighteen, we note that death holds the body, and hades (hell) holds the spirits. However, since Christ's resurrection, death briefly holds the bodies and hades does not hold the spirits of the saints. That compartment of hades has been emptied and they are with Christ. As Paul maintains in 2 Corinthians 5:8, "We are confident, I say, and willing rather to be absent from the body, and to be present with the Lord."

Other Names for Destinies

We need to mention here that there are other places of torment described in other terms: They are called pit, tartarus, gehenna, abyss and lake of fire. The word for hell is *hades* in the Greek; for death it is *thanator*; for tomb it is *mnenemeio* and for grave it is *tafos*.

Designations

In verse nineteen, John is to write "the things which thou hast seen." It is the vision that John had of Christ in chapter one. Then he is to write "the things which are," the church-age of chapter two and three and representing the whole church-age. And then the "things which shall be hereafter," which deal with things after the church-age. The seven stars of verse twenty are the angels or messengers or overseers of the churches. The seven candlesticks (Greek: lampstands) are the seven churches.

The Number Seven

Here we must consider the number "seven" as used in verse twenty of chapter one. It is referred to in nearly six hundred passages in the Bible. It means "totality" or "completeness." It is the greatest conceivable fullness of force. It can be placed under four headings:

Ritual

A. *Ritual use* deals with the seven days of the week. Mention must be made of the seven feast days of the Feast of Tabernacles of Leviticus 23:34. "Speak unto the children of Israel, saying, the fifteenth day of this seventh month shall be the feast of tabernacles for seven days unto the Lord." The Mosaic law prescribed seven he-lambs for festal offerings. Numbers 28:11 says: "And in the beginnings of your months ye shall offer a burnt offering unto the Lord: two young bullocks, and one ram, seven lambs of the first year without spot."

Historical

B. *The historical use.* Here one can mention the seven years of service of Jacob for Rachel. Genesis

29:18: "And Jacob loved Rachel: and said, I will serve thee seven years for Rachel thy younger daughter." We can also mention the seven years plenty and seven years famine of Genesis 41:29-30a: "Behold, there come seven years of plenty throughout all the land of Egypt; and there shall arise after them seven years of famine." One might also mention Samson's seven-day marriage feast and of course the seven-day march about Jericho. Then also seven years of tribulation of Revelation.

Literary

C. *The literary use.* Here we have the seven-fold curse predicted for Cain. Genesis 4:15 says: "And the Lord said unto him, therefore whosoever slayeth Cain, vengeance shall be taken on him seven-fold." Also the praise of God seven times a day: "Seven times a day do I praise thee because of thy righteous judgments" (Ps. 119:164). And the seven-fold forgiveness must also be mentioned. Luke 17: "And if he trespass against thee seven times in a day, and seven times in a day turn again to thee, saying, I repent; thou shalt forgive him."

Seven Again

D. Mention must be made of the numerous times "seven" is used in the Book of Revelation. There are the seven churches, the seven golden candlesticks, the seven stars, the seven angels of the churches, the seven spirits of God, a book of seven seals, a lamb with seven horns, seven angels with seven trumpets, seven thunders, seven last plagues, seven golden bowls, and a scarlet-coloured beast with seven heads. All show completeness.

Iniquity

There are also three forms of iniquity judged in Revelation.

1. The common sins of mankind. They are idolatry, lust and violence. The first deals with gods of wood, stone and metal. The second deals with a sensuous appetite or animal desire or passion. The third is the exercise of physical force.

2. Another sin is the awful atheistic blasphemy of the wild beast of Revelation 13, the antichrist.

3. And thirdly is the corrupt ecclesiasticism of an apostate church. Ecclesiasticism means a body of persons who administrate the affairs. Apostate means giving up the right faith and principles. Man awaits the permission of religion to indulge himself in the sin he loves. We are in this period of time. We do what comes naturally, according to inclination, through covetousness.

The professing church is tempted along the same old lines, pride, self-help and fleshly indulgence as well as lust and idolatry.

Sins of Our Day

We may name some of the above-named sins of our day. Independence is one. It is a getting of power. It includes murder, robbery and, one might add, a driving craze. There is also a sensuous appetite for other men or women. We are also experiencing a drive for pornography and a care-less spending spree on the part of governments and private citizens, on a credit rating basis. We are urged to invest on easy credit. Men and women are on drugs, and the Church is not immune. The use of blasphemy and cursing on radio and T.V. is not isolated.

Our Own Deeds

Before we consider chapters two and three of Revelation, we need to examine our own cravings and motivations and deeds in the light of Christ's lowly birth, life, death and purpose. What do we hope to achieve in the world? What is our aim, and main objective? What is our blessed hope? Paul, in writing to Titus (2:13), says: "Looking for that blessed hope, and the glorious appearing of the great God and our Saviour Jesus Christ." Our hope is not salvation. We have that and need not hope for what we have. Our hope is the coming of Christ. When (if dead) our bodies will be raised and (if alive) our bodies will be changed and given immortality, then we need not be ashamed at His coming. 1 John 2:28 says: "And now, little chil-dren, abide in him; that, when he shall appear, we may have confidence, and not be ashamed before him at his coming."

REVELATION 2-3

The Seven Churches

The Church Age

We now turn to Christ's messages to the seven churches and have these represent as well the church-age in historic fashion. About one eighth of the revelation is taken up with these seven messages to the churches. God emphasizes these messages and so must we.

The things that are, the messages to the churches, search us out in a most peculiar way. They ought to help us to purify our thinking and our lifestyle, to sort out what we are really after.

THE CHURCH AT EPHESUS

The first message is addressed to the church at Ephesus. It is the church at the end of the apostolic age. It was the capital of Asia Minor. Paul and Timothy founded the church in three years (Acts 19-20). Ephesus represents the church of the first century. Paul had eradicated sorcery, pride and the worship of Diana, their goddess. Paul had replaced these with repentance, faith, humility, watchfulness and joy in the Christian people. He had especially emphasized "first love." Together with love, he had promoted fellowship and unity. Ephesians 4:2-3 says: "With all lowliness and meekness, with longsuffering, forbearing one another in love; Endeavoring to keep the unity of the Spirit in the bond of peace."

Christ the Head of the Church

Christ shows what the Church looks like in His eyes. The things hid from us are known to Him. He is the Head of the Church. Christ directs and addresses the messenger (angel – leader) of the Church. We must note at the direction "to write," that no earthly man can write to an angel. We consider him to be a messenger or leader of the Church. Christ walks in the midst of the Church. The Church is not the building but the congregation of Christians. Christ is present, although unseen. If we realized that, would we be more careful of what we say or do in our assemblies?

The Works

In verse two Jesus says He knows the works, the labour and the patience of the congregation and He commends it for these qualities. It was an active, working, busy church; patient in suffering and they were holy and did not tolerate liars. Ministerial courtesy had no place in the Ephesian church. The false was eliminated. But one must go a little deeper. To the church at Thessalonica, Paul had emphasized certain other qualities. They are enumerated in 1 Thessalonians 1:3: "Remembering without ceasing your *work of faith*, and *labour of love*, and *patience of hope* in our Lord Jesus Christ, in the sight of God and our Father." These qualities were: "A work of faith; a labour of love; and a patience of hope." The Ephesian church had "work," "labour" and "patience." The qualifying elements were missing – "faith," "love" and "hope." These complement each other and are essential for a well-rounded character.

Meager Efforts

One must be aware of the meager efforts noticed and praised by Jesus in verse three. But it must all be done "for My name's sake." Unless our efforts bring glory to Him, they are in vain or useless. To suffer steadily is more difficult than to serve well.

Somewhat

Verse four has a sad aspect. "Nevertheless I have somewhat against thee, because thou hast left thy first love." The word "nevertheless" or "but" proves that He sees the things we do for Him and He also tests the motives that lie behind what we do. For what are we investing our time, talent and life? Is it for gain of self or is it because we love Him?

Disaffection

He does not say, "because you have *lost* your first love," but he does say, "Because you have *left* your first love." We do this by an act of the will. We become careless and begin to love something else more. The Lord is referring to *agape* love, a divine love and a reciprocal love moving alternately backward and forward like the expression used by

John: "We love Him because He first loved us" (1 John 4:19).

Consider a young woman who got married. She works harder than ever before because she loves him for whom she works. They embrace before he leaves for work and she waits for his home coming. But as the days go by, she becomes preoccupied with details. She watches less for him. She calls goodbye from an upstairs window.

Work Rather Than Christ

This was the situation of the church at Ephesus. Work was her concern rather than Him, and the freshness of love was ebbing. It was so with Martha and Mary. Martha received Jesus into her house. She was cumbered about much serving while Mary sat at Jesus' feet and heard His word. Martha complained that Mary was not serving. Jesus said: "Martha, thou are careful and troubled about many things: but one thing is needful: and Mary has chosen that good part, which shall not be taken away from her" (Luke 10:38-42). Perhaps, to a certain degree, that *agape* love is overtaken by *eros*, a natural, fleshly love, or even *phileo*, a brotherly love. No one and nothing must take the place of our love for Jesus. Not even religion must take His place, nor our family, nor home, nor wealth.

Repentance

The Ephesian church was evidently a falling assembly (vs. 5). "Repent," says Jesus. Repentance is a changed state of the soul. Our coldness and neglect must be broken up. Here, in verse five, it is not a call to "Christian service" but the "first works" are a giving of affection to Christ. Not what we do, but what we are is important to Christ. Christ and our relationship to Him must be our first concern.

Judgment

Jesus comes as He came to Sodom, in judgment. He will withdraw the Holy Spirit and darkness will follow and the privilege to witness will be changed. Ephesus today is a ruined archway; a moslem dwelling among desolate hills, we are told. There is no witness here where Paul laboured three years, night and day with tears. Acts 20:31: "Therefore watch, and remember that by the space of three years I ceased not to warn every one night and day with tears."

A discussion of "Nicolaitanism" will be taken up in a consideration of the church of Pergamos. Jesus notes every feeble effort we make in the matter of a terrible evil. If we have the least jealousy of love for our blessed Lord, He notes it and that is comforting to His children.

The Responsibility of Ears

The Church is to take notice of what Jesus says. He, therefore, places emphasis on the importance of the "ears." The ears are instruments of hearing. They are God's gift to human beings. We honour Him by listening to His words. He says in Mark 13:31, "Heaven and earth shall pass away: but my words shall not pass away." The Holy Spirit speaks through the Word. How we ought to thank God for our ears to hear His Word.

A Promise

Here is the promise to the Overcomer. There are those who overcome and those who are overcome. But the overcomer may eat of the tree of life which is in the midst of the paradise of God (Rev. 2:7). When Adam sinned, he was shut out from the garden lest he eat from the fruit of the tree of life and live forever in a sinful state. This tree, in the garden of Eden, seemingly sustained humanity in physical immortality against bodily dissolution. In the last Adam (Jesus) we have eternal life as to our spirits, and we look forward to bodily incorruptibility. This church could represent the church-age of A.D. 70-A.D. 170.

THE CHURCH AT SMYRNA

The City

Smyrna was a city of about 250,000 and the church there suffered a great persecution about A.D. 316. Verse eight speaks of Him who became dead and lived again. How fitting. The Church was cursed by false Jews and some Christians were killed. It is said that the ruler, Timur, wanted to build a tower of skulls. Jesus knows the Church's tribulation and affliction and poverty. He, too, had no place to lay His head. "But you are rich" with spiritual riches and one might behold these Christians "as gold refined by fire."

Judaism

The devil (Satan) worked against Christ in Judaism. The Jewish theologians should have recognized Jesus through the prophetic word. They pretended to observe the Law and thought they knew the way to heaven, but were blind leaders of the blind. They hallowed the Sabbath and failed to accept the Lord of the Sabbath. Jesus said to such Jews, "ye are of your father, the devil." They were Jews outwardly but not inwardly. Jews, if born again, belong to the Church. But as a nation, their time will come, when as a nation, they will repent and be recognized in a covenant relationship. God has always kept a remnant to be true to Him.

The early church was always in danger of becoming judaized. There was a great appeal for a visible temple, the Law (ritual), the priesthood and a glorious history. The Jews made a great impression upon the Gentiles. But these in Revelation and in Smyrna were lying Jews, for salvation is by grace and not of the Law or works. These Jews denied Christ's resurrection and His miracles as if wrought by Satan. They rejected the mighty works wrought after Pentecost in the name of Jesus. The liberal Jew must be carefully screened today. All that this shows is that an "earthly religion" is more attractive than a "heavenly walk."

Suffering and Encouragement

Christ says, "Do not fear the things you are about to suffer." God allows the devil to do certain things. The devil (through his followers) will cast some Christians of this church into prison. It is so true here that "the trial of your faith worketh patience."

"Ye shall have ten days tribulation." The early church here had ten great persecutions under Roman emperors, beginning with Nero and ending with Diocletian, whose last persecution, the most terrible, lasted just ten years. The catacombs, even today, remind us of persecutions.

Faithfulness

The Lord asks the Church to be "faithful unto death." This is to the point of martyrdom. And the crown of life is promised them. And we must ask ourselves: What is our resolve as Christians? Is it to obtain a crown or is it because we love Christ?

Appeal to the Ear

Again, the appeal to the ear. Not all would hear in the days of terrible trial. If Christians today were put to the test, would they be killed for their possessions or because they are Christians and witness for their Lord? Are our ears tuned for the coming of Christ?

Works in the Fire

Verse eleven show that the saints may be executed and may suffer the first death of those who "kill the body." Over these the "second death" has no authority. Revelation 20:6a says: "Blessed and holy is he that hath part in the first resurrection: on such the second death hath no power." The real believer has been judged on Calvary. All that is required is to examine his works, but not as sin – only in terms of worth, to be burned if worthless. We need to examine our works and see if there are any that will be burned.

Myrrh

The name Smyrna comes from the Ionic Greek for "myrrh," a sweet smelling gum in common use.

The Smyrna church represents the martyrs, and the fragrance of their affection fills the whole house of God. Let us meditate on Foxe's book of martyrs.

THE PERGAMOS CHURCH

The City

Revelation 2:12 shows a place where idolatry flourished under imperial favour. Such a church, in such a city of the world, might court the favour of the world. The kingdom of Pergamum became a Roman province in B.C. 130. It was a rival of Ephesus in the temples of Zeus and Athena. It was the first city in Asia (A.D. 29) with a temple for the worship of Augustus. This church could represent the church period of A.D. 316 to the end of that time period. It is a sad day when a church courts the favour of the world by being everything to everybody, and by accepting favours for which they must obligate themselves.

A Sword of Two Edges

Jesus begins His discourse by revealing the sword with two edges. It denotes stern judgment. The Ephesian church had a problem with first love. The Smyrna church had a problem with Satan's opposition and Jewish persuasion to accept empty laws. Here in this church, we recognize Constantine's embracing of Christianity, at about 313 A.D. The enemy would now try to defile what Satan could not destroy. But in this region paganism and the new Caesar-worship was rampant.

Territorial Aims

Verse thirteen says they lived where Satan is. The devil is not as yet in hell. He is the prince of this world, the god of this age. He directs his rulers of darkness here and in the air. Pergamos was a university city. At this time some prominent citizens acquired the title "Pontifex Maximus" which relates to "chief bridge-builders" and could refer to one who spans the gap between morals and Satan. It carries the thought of a Christian placing himself at the disposal of the world.

A Steadfast Church

Pergamos was one of the cities that contended for the privilege of worshiping the emperor, but the church there held fast to Christ even amidst persecution – even when a faithful witness, by the name of Antipas, was killed. It shows how the world reveals its animosity against Christianity. Jesus held the title "faithful witness" (1:5) and He bestows that title on Antipas, His child (2:13). What a profound meaning that has for all of us.

Careful Assessment

Then in verse fourteen, Jesus states what He has against the church. We would do well to ask ourselves, "What would He say to our church?" And of greater consideration, "What would He have against me as an individual Christian?" Over against their faithfulness stands the fact of "tolerating of evil." A party in the church that resisted emperor-worship, to the death in the case of Antipas, was yet caught in the insidious wiles of the Nicolaitans which the church in Ephesus withstood. These early Gnostics practiced licentiousness as a principle since they were not under law, but under grace. Paul, in Romans 6:15, says: "What then? Shall we sin, because we are not under the law, but under grace? God forbid." In such a position, we need to carefully assess and weigh the facts as facts.

Balaam

Here we become acquainted with the doctrine of Balaam as given in Numbers 25:1-3. "And Israel abode in Shittim, and the people began to commit whoredom with the daughters of Moab. And they called the people unto the sacrifices of their gods: and the people did eat, and bowed down to their gods. And Israel joined himself unto Baal-peor: and the anger of the Lord was kindled against Israel." The prophet taught Balak, the king, to corrupt the people who could not be cursed. He counselled this king of Moab to entice Israel into Moab heathen idolatry, bringing death by plague on 24,000 Israelites. Satan, failing to disrupt the church by persecution in Smyrna days, persuades some members to adopt idolatry and commit fornication. "To eat things sacrificed to idols" is to feast in the idol's temple. Outside, saints could buy whatever they needed, even though it had been previously offered to idols. 1 Corinthians 10:25 says: "Whatsoever is sold in the shambles, that eat, asking no question for conscience sake."

Two Cups

In Pergamos some sought to drink the cup of the Lord and the cup of demons and so provoke the Lord. We need to ask, "What could be compared to idolatry in the church of today? Might one name fleshly license or liberality in copying worldly standards and methods? The definition for "fornication" is voluntary sexual intercourse between male and female. Today this evil needs a definition of enlargement. We have this evil in our schools, businesses, police force and even in church. It may even, to a certain extent, be practiced by some as a form of doctrine.

Nicolaitans

Verse fifteen reveals another evil present. Ephesus had the works of the Nicolaitans, but hated them. Here the works and their teaching were tolerated. Here the question may arise: Should the minority call something good and acceptable because the majority decides in favour? There seems to be no record of such a section in the early church. We must get the meaning from the name. It comes from *nikao* (to conquer) and *laos* (people), and it consequently means "the rulers of the laity," a priestly cast corresponding to the Levites in Israel. It ignores the priesthood of all believers. It ignores what Matthew says in Matthew 23:8-10: "But be not ye called Rabbi: for one is your Master, even Christ; and all ye are brethren. And call no man your father upon the earth: for one is your Father, which is in heaven. Neither be ye called masters: for one is your Master, even Christ."

Loving Counsel

Christ gives them loving counsel: repent, change and turn around. The deeper the evil, the more difficult is the self-judgment. A proper question for self-judgment would be: Do we ever find ourselves guilty?

How Far Can One Go?

What follows in verse sixteen has nothing to do with the Lord's coming for His own, but, rather, it has to do with a coming in judgment upon the sinners here for their sin. It is like the angel of the Lord who stood with his drawn sword against the mad prophet, Balaam, in Israel days. The sword could be the word that convicts them. How does one excuse oneself to the Holy Spirit for what one wants to do, knowing beforehand that such action is wrong? Should a pastor preach the truth even though it may cause someone to leave the assembly of believers?

A Promise

Here, in verse seventeen, is the promise to overcomers. The word "hidden" may refer to the wilderness manna which was preserved for a memorial in the ark of the covenant. Exodus 16:33 says: "And Moses said unto Aaron, take a pot, and put an Omer full of manna therein, and lay it up before the Lord, to be kept for your generations." Jesus also said in John 6:33, "For the bread of God is he which cometh down from heaven, and giveth life unto the world." Christ is the true bread from heaven, and that may be the idea here. Those faithful to Christ will have intimate and transcendent fellowship with Him. These Pergamos believers were to realize that secret relationship into which the heavenly saints are brought by the Spirit while on earth. The world is not aware of this blessed relationship. It exceeds the Babylonian system of idolatry.

A White Stone

Verse seventeen speaks also of a "white stone." Christ gives every member of His body something. Some capacity that no other member has. Every believer knows the Lord a little differently, at least in some measure. It gives each one a personal character, just as each one has a different facial expression.

A New Name

A new name would indicate the recipient's own name intermingled with Christ's name and character – which makes for a new name. It is a revelation of his everlasting title. It denotes what glory one has; what intimate relationship one has with his Lord – all by himself, alone with his Lord. When I contemplated this personal, wonderful relationship with the Lord, I broke out in loud weeping, in sorrow for what I am lacking and for joy for what I can become in Christ.

Names of Meaning

Think of the names of John the Baptist as "one sent, a forerunner." Think of Abraham as the "man of faith." Jacob as "Israel." Paul as a "chosen vessel." Peter as "a rock." Jesus as the "Lamb of God,

Saviour, Redeemer." Only we, as personal beings, and Christ know what we *are* and *shall be*, and even then we shall be surprised at our new name given by Christ and known only by the one receiving it. Therefore we must substantiate one life only by Christ – His holy and immaculate life.

THE CHURCH OF THYATIRA

Constant Worship

The church of Thyatira could represent a time period from about 500-1500 A.D., but was addressed by John early in Revelation. There was Apollo worship in this city which was under Roman domination. The word "Thyatira" means "constant worship."

Various Moods of Love

Here we have Christ in the most searching and terrible aspect of any He assumes toward the churches. That is what is evident in the expression "eyes like a flame of fire," in verse eighteen. It shows the "holy jealousy of infinite love." We need to contemplate the Final Solution of Love, and in that act of love we need to understand the various moods of love. These moods of divine love we find in the various dealings of God with the various sinners in Revelation. What we consider to be "rough punishment" may be a final solution, on the part of God, to the sin question.

Spurious Love

"His feet are like fine brass." The sinful act committed here is that another authority is permitted to supplant Christ. And so Christ stands in judgment, to *stamp* out that which would take His place. Christ will not tolerate adulterous love in our lives.

After Salvation

In verse nineteen, we have the necessary qualities after we have experienced salvation. They are works, love, service, faith and patience. These do not bring the experience of salvation but are needful after one has experienced salvation.

Jezebel

In verse twenty, Christ warns the church about allowing the woman Jezebel free reign. This could have been a literal woman whom the Lord calls by the name of Jezebel. In the Old Testament the woman Jezebel was the wife of King Ahab who worshiped idols. 1 Kings 21:25 says: "But there was none like unto Ahab, which did sell himself to work wickedness in the sight of the Lord, whom Jezebel his wife stirred up." She called herself a prophetess and wanted to take the place of the Holy Spirit, the Spirit who spoke not of Himself, but what He heard from the Lord. Later it could be the voice of a church which refers to herself as "the mother church." When a church claims she alone knows the voice of God, she is certainly mistaken and false. Human authority must not replace that of the Holy Spirit. One is puzzled to know how such a woman had so much shrewdness and sex appeal as to lead astray the servant of God in the church. But such vile acts occur even today among so-called Christians and pastors.

Indulgence

Her lusting spirit persuaded some to commit fornication. The confessional could arouse, within the person, the idea to stifle conscience and allow that person to indulge the flesh. An image, too, can replace Christ with something else. We must be careful that nothing but nothing replaces Christ in our lives.

Longsuffering

Verse twenty-one shows false religion giving liberty to lusts which the flesh loves. And yet, the Lord gives her time (space) to repent. How patient the Lord is. Peter speaks of this in 2 Peter 3:9: "The Lord is not slack concerning His promise, as some men count slackness; but is longsuffering to us-ward, not willing that any should perish, but that all should come to repentance." This word, "I gave her time," is an allusion to a definite visit or message of warning to this woman. But repentance and cessation, God's way, are a bitter pill to the flesh. And the Lord will change her bed of whoredom into a bed of anguish and sickness. Nor shall her children (descendants) live. No seed of such an abhorrent act must be allowed to function. It could develop into a system and have to be dealt with later, as in Revelation 17. The sad part is that others are affected and they, too, must be dealt with. And verse twenty-three shows that each will have a just dealing from the Lord. Each individual in the church must answer for himself.

Deep Things

Verse twenty-four shows the magicians from Babylon and Persia always extolling their knowledge of the "deep thing," their inner knowledge." Jesus calls it "depths of Satan." It originates with Satan. It is a spiritual affair where people ignore salvation in Christ which really is the "mystery of God in Christ." People seek peace of mind in transcendental meditation when they can only find it in Christ. And verse twenty-five encourages the faithful in the church to "hold fast what you have." It carries the meaning of "get a grip on" or "hold fast what you have." It also means "hold on as a single decisive effort." How easy it is to let the truth slip away and to become gullible and conformed and lukewarm. Let the faithful remain true until He comes.

Verse twenty-six warns Christians that it is not enough to deny Jezebel in doctrine and works, but "he that keepeth unto the end my works" is crowned at the end. Her works were unholy. His were holy.

Entrance Fee

Verses twenty-six and twenty-seven point to the coming millennial kingdom which is to be established by the Lord at His return to earth. Revelation 20:4 says: "And I saw thrones, and they sat upon them, and judgment was given unto them: and I saw the souls of them that were beheaded for the witness of Jesus, and for the word of God, and which had not worshiped the beast neither his image, neither had received his mark upon their foreheads, or in their hands: and they lived and reigned with Christ a thousand years." We do not enter the millennium by the new birth. The thousand year reign will come later. Here, those who overcome, shall accompany Christ in order to overthrow worldly power and shall reign with Him in His Kingdom. The Thyatira saints are representative of all the saints who shall judge the world with Him. Paul makes this point in 1 Corinthians 6:2a: "Do ye not know that the saints shall judge the world?" We should, therefore, be able to judge smaller matters at present. Brother going to law with brother. The "rod of iron" is actually the "royal sceptre. "We shall reign royally with Him.

The Star

Christ is the bright morning star. He is so named in Revelation 22:16b: "I am the root and the offspring of David, and the bright morning star." We are actually living in the night at present (spiritually speaking). The day will come when the morning star arises – the millennial reign will be the day for the overcomers. Thyatira represents all who in trials wait for the coming day – the Day of Christ.

THE CHURCH OF SARDIS

The City

Sardis was some thirty miles south-east of Thyatira. It was later conquered by Cyrus and then by Alexander the Great. Then in 214 B.C. it was taken by Antiochus the Great. The worship of Cybele was practiced and it was known as the city of softness, luxury and immorality. The church here could represent the church-age of the Reformation period, A.D. 1520-1750. The church can be likened unto a dying church. She is not growing in grace. A few, however, were faithful.

Examination

Verse one of chapter three shows the designation of the fullness of the Holy Spirit before the throne of God in heaven. The Spirit is subject to the Son as the Son to the Father, in the redemption arrangement. Although all are equal in the fact of Deity, Christ examines the church through the Spirit and through its leaders. What a responsibility these leaders have.

One Way

In this church-age history, Christ seems to deal with a dying Protestantism or professing Christianity as such – a mere profession that bears only the name. Think of the state churches with creeds, histories and influence but no experience of salvation; yoked to the world. Someone remarks that there are many ways of climbing into an upstairs house. It can be done by a tree or by a ladder or some other way. Christ says there is only *one* way to the heavenly Father. Jesus says: "I am the Way, the Truth and the Life; no one cometh unto the Father, but by Me" (John 14:6).

Not Perfect

Verse two shows the "works not perfect before God," neither in doctrine nor walk. Jesus did not say: "Arise from the dead," for these are vestiges of life although there is grave peril. Considering the church-age, the reformers did speak of "justification" by faith apart from works. But they did not stress "identification" at Calvary with Christ and with Christ's resurrection; dying with Christ and rising with Him in newness of life. This newness is not found in the gratification of the flesh, and the ordination of those of whom Paul speaks as "burned in their lust one toward another, men with men; and women did change the natural use into that which is against nature (Rom. 1:26-27).

God's Standard

In verses two and three are five commands to Sardis. Be watchful; strengthen the things that remain; remember your teaching; and hold fast and repent. Their works have not measured up to God's standard.

A Sacrament

Right here we must refer to the term "sacrament" as practiced by the church. It is a Babylonian expression. The Latin *sacramentum* is the word for a mystery of the pagan religion. It originates in the Chaldean mysteries. The Latin *sacrare* means "to make sacred," and is dedicated to some religious purpose; hallowed or made holy. To us baptism means a sign of commitment to Christ, and the Lord's Supper is a memorial feast of Christ's suffering.

Ordinances

In the Greek New Testament there is no word corresponding to sacrament. Nor does early

Christianity afford any trace of applying the term to certain rites of the church. It would be better to say "ordinances" of Christ; a command; a practice. Baptism and the Lord's Supper may also be termed "rites" of the church or a ceremony or a custom. Or it could be called "a ceremonial act or procedure." In the New Testament, the sacraments are presented as "a means of grace." Associated with baptism is *forgiveness*: "Then Peter said unto them, repent, and be baptized every one of you in the name of Jesus Christ for the remission of sins" (Acts 2:38a). Also *cleansing:* "That he might sanctify and cleanse it with the washing of water by the word" (Eph. 5:26). Also *spiritual quickening*: "Buried with him in baptism, wherein also ye are risen with him through the faith of the operation of God, who hath raised him form the dead" (Col. 2:12a). The Roman church holds that virtue and power are inherent in themselves. They communicate saving benefits to those who receive them. The Lutheran church resembles the Roman church in believing the above. Reformed or Evangelical churches teach that the efficacy of these rites lies not in themselves but in the blessing of Christ and the operation of the Holy Spirit and depends upon *faith* in the one who receives them.

A Permanent Deposit

Verse three tell the church to "keep in mind" that she has received as "a permanent deposit" that which they heard, and they must safeguard it and repent. If she does not watch, He will come as a thief in judgment. He wants His own to expect Him and His coming at any time. Jesus wants us to function, not as a social club but as His peculiar people. 1 Peter 2:9 says: "But ye are a chosen generation, a royal priesthood, an holy nation, a peculiar people; that ye should show forth the praises of him who hath called you out of darkness into his marvellous light." So many bear Christ's name but go nowhere and have no power or fruit. It is much ado about nothing.

God Sees and Knows All

Verse four reveals a fact that is not remembered always. It is the fact that the all-seeing eye of God knows and sees all. Here are a few names of overcomers. It is a faithful remnant, the minority. To them is the promise of fellowship with Christ. They love and adhere to His Word and they represent purity and receive the promise, "and they shall walk with me in white." This means a victorious righteousness for they are worthy. Of Enoch it was said: "And Enoch walked with God: and he was not; for God took him" (Gen. 5:24).

Names Written in Heaven

Verse five speaks of the divine register which first occurs in Exodus 32:32, where Moses asks to be blotted out of the book which God has written, if God will not forgive Israel's sin in making and worshiping the golden calf. Luke 10:20 refers to the joy of the disciples for their ability to perform miracles, and Jesus says: "Notwithstanding in this rejoice not, that the spirits are subject unto you; but rather rejoice, because your names are written in heaven." It is release from anxiety for overcomers. As Jesus says in Matthew 10:32, "Whosoever therefore shall confess me before men, him will I confess also before my Father which is in heaven." Jesus is our advocate. He pleads our cause before the Throne. Jesus is not an angel as some claim. He confesses us before the angels. In Luke 12:8 Jesus says: "Also I say unto you, Whosoever shall confess me before men, him shall the Son of man also confess before the angels of God."

Those Who Do Not Listen

To hear when all ears are deaf to the Holy Spirit is difficult. To serve when others mock and entertain worldly ideas also is difficult. Who would oppose those in Israel who were determined to worship a golden calf? Families were unable to oppose the methods employed by the communist government in Russia; they could only flee and even that escape route was later closed. What can be done about rulers who legalize abortion and force tax payers to underwrite the bill? Only God is able to deal with such.

THE PHILADELPHIA CHURCH

The City

This city is some twenty-eight miles south-east of Sardis. It is subject to earthquakes. Bacchus was the chief deity – the god of wine. It offered, later on, stubborn resistance to the Turks in A.D. 1340, and is now called Ala Sheher (reddish city because of red hills). It could represent church history A.D. 1750-1900.

The City of Brotherly Love

The name Philadelphia arouses our attention. It is the last time it occurs in the New Testament, and it is a Geek word. It appears in Scriptures such as Romans 12:10a: "Be kindly affectioned one to another with brotherly love." 1 Thessalonians 4:9a: "But as touching brotherly love ye need not that I write unto you." Hebrews 13:1a: "Let brotherly love continue." 2 Peter 1:7: "And to godliness brotherly kindness; and to brotherly kindness charity (love)." The word used here for love is *phileo* and for brother *adelphos*. It is the true church among the professing church.

Lord Over David's House

Verse seven shows that Christ is holy even if a church loses out. In Revelation 1:18, Jesus says: "I have the keys of death and of hades." Here He has the key of David. In the first statement He spoke of salvation as power and victory over death and the unseen world. In our text He announces His royal claims as Lord and Head of David's house and looks toward the Kingdom which He will establish on earth. Isaiah 65:24-25 speaks of this: "And it shall come to pass, that before they call, I will answer... the wolf and the lamb shall feed together, and the lion shall eat straw like the bullock... they shall not hurt nor destroy in all my holy mountain, saith the Lord." Jesus has exclusive power in heaven, earth and hades. In Matthew 28:18, Jesus says: "All power is given unto me in heaven and in earth." He can shut doors of sin and open doors of opportunity. He can establish and rule kingdoms. He is able also to open for us the doors for witnessing.

Three Qualities

Verse eight sets out the fact that Philadelphia did not have the energy of Ephesus, but she had three other qualities which were precious. She had "a little strength" (Greek: power); she "had kept His Word" and "had not denied His name." Therefore, He had set before her an open door. Here was a good opportunity for missionary effort in spite of the Jewish hostility.

Little But Tall And Great

Regarding the word "little" in verse eight, we must remember Zacchaeus who was little of stature but accomplished great ends. Luke 19:5 says: "And when Jesus came to the place, he looked up, and saw him, and said unto him, Zacchaeus, make haste, and come down; for today I must abide at thy house." And remember the Lord's company as "a little flock" (Luke 12:32). The Philadelphia assembly was unimportant in the eyes of the world. Perhaps they were few in number; poor in property and possessions; or even low in the social scale, but here is a living response to the known Word. They put into action what others only professed. Keeping His Word in some crisis or trial is what counts.

The Power of a Christian

Verse nine gives the promise that He will deal with Judaizing Christians who are causing friction among the true Christians. Jesus had said to the

Samaritan woman, "salvation is of the Jews" (John 4:22), but later He wept over Jerusalem, saying, "If thou hadst known, even thou, at least in this thy day, the things which belong unto thy peace! but now they are hid from thine eyes" (Luke 19:42). The last part of verse nine shows that the saints will judge the world and angels (1 Cor. 6:2), and this only because of Christ's special love for His own.

No Yielding

Verse ten is very important. Trial and testing brings temptation to yield. But Jesus did not yield to the devil. Matthew 4:10 says: "Then saith Jesus unto him, get thee hence, Satan: for it is written, Thou shalt worship the Lord thy God, and him only shalt thou serve." And Jesus will aid the church here in this trial. We are told there is still a church in Philadelphia in spite of the Turks. Here is what patience (Greek: endurance) can secure. "I will keep you *from*": the Greek word is *ek* and can mean "out of" the hour of trial. This hour, upon "all the inhabited earth," is seen in Revelation 13:7-8 in the career of the beast. It is to try the earth-dwellers whether they will follow Satan's false Christ or not. The Philadelphia believers are to be kept out of this hour. Like Enoch, kept out of the flood. Like Noah, representing Israel, kept "in" the flood.

Trial

This hour of trial, as the Greek has it (*peirasmou* – a proving), needs to be studied in the light of Daniel 12:1 that says: "And at that time shall

Michael stand up, the great prince which standeth for the children of thy people: and there shall be a *time of trouble*, such as never was since there was a nation even to that same time: and at that time thy people shall be delivered, everyone that shall be found written in the book." And Jesus speaks of this in Matthew 24:15a: "When ye therefore shall see the abomination of desolation, spoken of by Daniel the prophet, stand in the holy place, (whoso readeth, let him understand)." The expression "upon the whole earth" is the inhabited world of men.

Not Appointed to Wrath

Two Greek words denote tribulation. One is *orge* and the other is *thlipsis*. The latter means general suffering as in Matthew 24:9a. Jesus says: "Then shall they deliver you up to be afflicted, and shall kill you." The word *orge* means divine wrath, as in Matthew 3:7 where John the Baptist says to the Pharisees and Sadducees, "But when he saw many of the Pharisees and Sadducees come to his baptism, he said unto them, O generation of vipers, who hath warned you to flee from the *wrath to come*?" In John 3:36, James 1:19 and Rev. 6:16-17, it denotes divine wrath, the period of tribulation. It is reaction against sin, but we who are in Christ are not appointed unto wrath. Paul wrote to the church of Thessalonica in 1 Thessalonians 5:9: "For God hath not appointed us to *wrath*, but to obtain salvation by our Lord Jesus Christ."

A Difference

We must note a difference between the Church and Israel. Since Pentecost the Holy Spirit has sealed the Church. The function of the Church is to gather in local assemblies, have various ministries and proclaim the gospel. Her future is to be caught up to be with her Lord and the New Jerusalem. 1 John 3:2 says: "Beloved, now are the sons of God, and it doth not yet appear what we shall be: but we know that, when He shall appear, we shall be like Him; for we shall see Him as He is." Israel has its origin with Abraham. Membership in Israel is by birth and affiliation with beliefs, ritual and practices of Judaism. Israel's future is pictured in Matthew 23:39. "For I say unto you, Ye shall not see me henceforth, till ye shall say, Blessed is he that cometh in the name of the Lord." Israel has an earthly mission and this is worked out on earth. Therefore, the Church has no place in the prophecy of Daniel: "Seventy weeks are determined upon *thy people* and upon *thy holy city*, to finish the transgression, and to make an end of sins" (Dan. 9:24a). It is for Daniel's people. The seventy weeks are for Israel and the nations. Daniel's people shall experience the tribulation. That is the reason that the church is mentioned in Revelation 2-3 but is not mentioned in Revelation 4-18. From Thyatira on, the eyes of saints are directed to the Lord's return as the only hope. The time is coming when, "if the days were not shortened, no man should be saved" (Matt. 24:22).

God's Time

To the Lord "time" is a passing thing. One thousand years is as one day. Hence the expression, "I come quickly." The Lord deals with "history" not just a human life in its brevity. In all of that which passes and is fleeting, we are to "hold fast" to our spiritual possessions. There is real danger that we can lose them – such as holiness, purity, interest, the Word, prayer. The reward of a crown is assured those who hold fast. The crown is a reward, it is not "eternal life." Eternal life is a gift according to Revelation 2:10. In 2 Timothy 4:8a, we read: "Henceforth there is laid up for me a crown of righteousness," and in James 1:12 we read: "Blessed is the man that endureth temptation; for when he is tried he shall receive the crown of life." The "pillar" in verse twelve shows establishment forever or being firmly fixed spiritually. Here is permanency, strength, beauty. Fixity of character is at last achieved, "and he shall go no more out." Let us look at the various crowns as rewards.

Crowns

1. *The crown of rejoicing* of the soul winner. Paul writes to the Thessalonian church in this way: "For what is our hope or joy, or crown of rejoicing? Are not even ye in the presence of our Lord Jesus Christ at his coming?"

2. *The crown of righteousness.* Paul writes to Timothy on this wise: "Henceforth there is laid up for me a crown of righteousness, which the Lord, the righteous judge, shall give me at that day" (2 Tim. 4:8a).

3. *The crown of glory.* Peter writes about this in 1 Peter 5:4: "And when the chief shepherd shall appear, ye shall receive a crown of glory, that fadeth not away."

4. *The crown of life.* James 1:12 speaks of such a crown. "Blessed is the man that endureth temptation: for when he is tried, he shall receive the crown of life, which the Lord hath promised to them that love him."

A New Name

Verse twelve shows the saint receiving the triple name, "Of God," "Of the city of God" and "Of Christ," on his forehead, just as the high priest wore the name of Jehovah upon his forehead. The new name is proof of ownership by God, as a citizen of the New Jerusalem, with the new symbol of the glorious personality of Christ in contrast with the mark of the beast.

Since this is the one church where Christ promises to "keep her out of the hour of trial," we must consider certain other facts that are related to a translation.

When Jesus comes back to establish His Kingdom, in Revelation 19, the destruction of the wicked is described (vs. 17-21). The beast and false prophet are cast into the lake of fire and the rest are slain. In Revelation 20, Satan is bound for a thousand years. Mention is made of the resurrection of the tribulation saints who were martyred and the thousand years will run their course and end in the Great White Throne judgment. But *no* mention is made of a "translation."

When Christ comes for His disciples, they will go *from* earth to heaven. When Christ comes to set up His Kingdom on earth, the very opposite occurs. They will come *from* heaven to earth.

Now there is no "translation" of the saints in

the Old Testament except possibly Enoch and Elijah, and until the New Testament there is no prophetic declaration that Christ is coming *for* the living saints.

The Last Trump

Let us also say that the "last trump" in 1 Corinthians 15:52 has no reference to the angelic trumpets of Revelation. It is a trumpet of resurrection and translation and not of judgment of unbelievers. In 1 Thessalonians 4:13-18 we have these words:

To Meet the Lord

"But I would not have you to be ignorant, brethren, concerning them which are asleep, that ye sorrow not, even as others which have no hope. For if we believe that Jesus died and rose again, even so them also which sleep in Jesus will God bring with Him. For this we say unto you by the word of the Lord, that we which are alive and remain unto the coming of the Lord shall not prevent them which are asleep. For the Lord himself shall descend from heaven with a shout, with the voice of the archangel, and with the trump of God: and the dead in Christ shall rise first; Then we which are alive and remain shall be caught up together with them in the clouds, to meet the Lord in the air: and so shall we ever be with the Lord. Wherefore comfort one another with these words."

A Question

How could Paul extend his comfort to the Thessalonians if they had first to pass through the wrath of the tribulation? This hope is based on certain deliverance from the wrath of God. The Day of the Lord comes as a thief in the night and unexpected. This day includes the millennium in judgment and in Matthew 24 there are many *signs* of the coming Kingdom, but in connection with the rapture, not a sign is given. We are to watch and be sober.

Christ Himself will receive a "new" name along with all else in the future world. That new name remains a mystery (Rev. 3:12).

THE CHURCH OF LAODICEA

The City

This city was about forty miles south-east of Philadelphia and some forty miles east of Ephesus. It is the last of the seven churches addressed. It was the great trade route to the east and was the seat of large manufacturing and banking operations. The worship of Asklepios was practiced. It was the home of many Jews and was known as "the city of compromise," or "justice of the people." The church here is now a deserted ruin. Here is the final state of apostasy – a falling away, indifference, carelessness. She could represent the church or the end time. The name comes from the Greek *laos* (people) and *dikas* (to rule). It means "the rule of the people" – each does as seems right to him.

Lukewarm

Verse fourteen shows that the lukewarm church has failed, but Christ remains the same.

His is "the faithful and true witness," and Christ is *not* the first of creatures, as some claim. He is the originating source of creation through whom God works. Paul, writing to the Colossian church, says: "Who is the image of the invisible God, the firstborn of every creature: And he is the head of the body, the church: who is the beginning, the firstborn from the dead; that in all things he might have the preeminence (Col. 1:15,18). Jesus can also keep us, if we are faithful, despite the failure of the church as an organization, as for instance the World Council of Churches.

Verse fifteen says the church is neither hot nor cold. She is lukewarm and has no real concern for Christ. Some signs of lukewarmness in churches may be named:

A. No concern to serve.

B. No concern about worship.

C. No concern about souls.

D. No concern about behaviour in the house of God.

Separation

Verse sixteen shows Christ separating Himself, disassociating Himself from such who are careless professors. He was not thrust out, He withdrew. Of such a church it is true: "Be sure your sin will find you out." And as He says in our text, "I will spew (Greek: vomit) thee out of my mouth."

The Condition (Situation)

Here we see the "spiritual state" of the church. In verse seventeen we see that she is self-confident, ignorant of her true condition and her imminent danger. She says: "I am rich and increased with goods." Here is a church which carries the pride of wealth into her spiritual life. She imagined spiritual riches which she did not possess. She was rich in pride and conceit and self-complacency. Could we apply the term "wealth" today? Affording a number of cars, amusement, furniture, comfort and leisure?

Double-mindedness

This leads to an effort to do both – to serve Christ somehow and somewhat and to also hang on by any means to the world and what it can offer. 2 Timothy 3:1-5 states this clearly: "This know also, that in the last days perilous times shall come. For men shall be lovers of their own selves, covetous (money lovers), boasters, proud, blasphemers, disobedient to parents, unthankful, unholy, without natural affection, trucebreakers, false accusers, incontinent, fierce, despisers of those that are good, traitors, heady, highminded, lovers of pleasures more than lovers of God; Having a form of godliness, but denying the power thereof: from such turn away." One needs only to think of such pastors who possess million dollar vacation homes, and when one of them was said "to be raised on the golf course," he answered, "God's people have a right to prosper." He forgot about Jesus' poverty and the martyrs of the past.

Spiritual Poverty

There is no sense of need. There is drowsiness that needs no salvation or perhaps just a semblance of salvation. It's a church that can easily get along with a formal or worldly standard, and the harm is spiritual poverty and carnality. The motto is: "Let us do what comes naturally." That is one reason why Paul says: "We have no confidence in the flesh" (Phil. 3:3).

Satisfaction Unsatisfied

It is a sad situation when a church is absolutely satisfied with her condition. Laodicea has need of nothing and does not perceive that she is wretched and miserable, and poor and blind and naked. This need not be construed as the same state in which Adam and Eve found themselves in before the fall. These Laodiceans willfully ignored moral accountability – like nudists who try to get back to the Garden of Eden situation by their own efforts. Innocency can only be obtained through Christ, and even then common sense (a sensible morality) must prevail. Genesis 3:21 says: "Unto Adam also and to his wife did the Lord God make coats of skins, and clothed them."

Putting Off the Old Man

In verse eighteen, Jesus is willing to help. He says: "buy of me gold tried in the fire." It cost Jesus to try the fires of hell to redeem the church. To be tested and found "steadfast" is to be rich. The white raiment is the righteousness of the saints, that our "former self" be not seen. Revelation 19:8 shows this to be true: "And to her was granted that she should be arrayed in fine linen, clean and white: for the fine linen is the righteousness of saints." It is the "putting off the old." These Laodiceans were trying to "drag" the old man along behind, and that makes for "luke-warmness" in Christians.

The ancient eyesalve first smarted and then healed and soothed. So the Holy Spirit convicts, then guides and comfort.

Chastening

Verse nineteen says that Jesus rebukes and chastens. The word "chaste" denotes purity or decency. "Chasten" implies restraint or purifying, like love in child training for betterment of the one trained. Right here we must take note of the sad account of one of the tribes of Israel as given in Hosea 4:17, which states: "Ephraim is joined to idols: let him alone." The day of grace for that tribe was past; there was no repentance.

Outside the Door

Then in verse twenty we have Christ's final plea to the individual. Jesus, having been shut out from the fellowship of the general assembly, stands outside at the door and knocks. He is patient, loving and forgiving to anyone willing to break with carelessness, lukewarmness and apostasy. Jesus extends the plea of deepest concern. He only knows the terrible reward for rejection. His children must not play with sin. God will not spare. He did not spare His own Son. Eternal security must take into account the severity of the justice of God.

A Two-Way Deal

Even in their final fellowship, Jesus makes it a two-way deal. "I will eat with him and he with me."

That is reciprocate love. Here is Love's Final Solution. There is no trace of selfishness. It is above the love-life between husband and wife. There are no vagrancies (wanderings) or variables (change, deviation) here. To sit with Christ upon His throne is a privilege reserved only for the "pure in heart." Here, the highest place is within the reach of the lowest. Here is Christ's most tender plea for He knows how difficult it is to overcome – to be tested and tried in all points. John, in 1 John 5:4, says: "And this is the victory that overcometh... even our faith." By faith one must step out of any questionable assembly and follow Him.

Voices and His Voice

The world is full of voices today, calling to us to listen to what man is, has done and will do. But such voices grow silent and pass. The promise of Christ stands the test of time. History has proven that. The Church is undergoing changes in our day and one wonders what the Church will be like by the time Christ appears. Let us heed the warning, "If the days were not shortened, there should no flesh be saved" (Matt. 24:22). Since we are endowed with ears, let us hear and be ready for His coming.

The Church

Since we have dealt with the churches, we need to define the church and see what she stands for. The word "church" is the Greek word *Ecclesia* meaning an assembly of "called out ones." The Greek word *Ecclesia* corresponds with the Latin word *Congregatio* which is the English word "congregation," an assembly of Christians gathered for worship. Collectively, it is the whole body of born-again Christians scattered throughout the earth.

She had her inception on the day of Pentecost when Jesus said to Peter: "Thou art Peter, and upon this rock I will build my church" (Matt. 16:18). The word for Peter is "Petros" and the other word for "upon this rock," is "Petra." It would say, "Peter you are a piece of the Rock upon whom the church is built."

The church is not a Jewish Dispensation. The Jews, as a nation, are on a sidetrack at this time, except those who accept Jesus and belong to the Church. Matthew 13 has them as "a treasure hidden." Blindness has come to them until the "fullness of the Gentiles have come in." Romans 11:25 says: "For I would not, brethren, that ye should be ignorant of this mystery, lest ye should be wise in your own conceits; that blindness in part is happened to Israel, until the fullness of the Gentiles be come in."

Nor is the Church the Kingdom. There can be no kingdom until the nobleman farmer, who is in a far country receiving the kingdom, returns. Luke 19:12 says: "He said therefore, a certain nobleman went into a far country to receive for himself a kingdom, and to return."

A Mystery

The church is a mystery. Ephesians 3:4-6 reads: "Whereby, when we read, ye may understand my knowledge in the mystery of Christ. Which in other ages was not made known unto the sons of men, as it is now revealed unto his holy apostles and prophets by the Spirit; That the Gentiles should be fellow heirs, and of the same body, and partakers of his promise in Christ by the gospel." She is a called out body. Israel is a nation. The Church consists of people from all nations. The Church is also the body of Christ. Ephesians 1:22 says: "And hath put all things under his feet, and gave him to be the head over all things to the church... which is his body." The Church is also the Bride of Christ, at present a virgin: "That I may present you as a chaste virgin to Christ" (2 Cor. 11:2b). She is now being prepared, then given. We shall be like Him. There is a saying in the German language as *"gleich and gleich gesellt sich,"* which carries the meaning, "like and like has a common bond."

The Church's Origin

The origin of the Church according to Ephesians 1:4 is before the foundation of the world. In Revelation 19:9 some are called to the marriage of the Lamb. However, the Bride is not called, she has a right to be present. Those called must be friends, as John the Baptist was.

The Church's Mission

The mission of the Church is to proclaim the gospel, the good news. "Go ye, therefore, into all the world" (Mark 16:15).

The Church's Destiny

The destiny of the Church is to be "caught up" like Enoch before the flood. The tribulation is not for the perfecting of the saints. It is "Jacob's Trouble." Jeremiah 30:7 says: "Alas! for that day is great, so that none is like it: it is even the time of Jacob's trouble; but he shall be saved out of it."

The Church's Judgment

The judgment of the Church is found according to 2 Corinthians 5:10. Let us be ready for His coming and for the marriage of the Lamb. The judgment of the Church is at the judgment seat of Christ.

The Things Which Shall Be Hereafter

Hereafter

In the Scripture here we have the "things which shall be hereafter." The word "hereafter" speaks of a time after the church-age or after the rapture, if you will. For that reason a door is opened in heaven. It is opened because of God's grace and love and opportunity that has been extended to John as a representative of the Church, to see what God has prepared for His own.

A Door

The word "Door" could mean "entrance" or "gate" or "opening." The professing church having failed and having been rejected as God's house, must be superseded (replaced) by the coming of the Lord and His Kingdom. So John is shown now what comes after the church-age. And it is pronounced by the "first" voice in Revelation 1:10, and it is also pronounced in 1 Thessalonians 1:10 – Jesus delivering His own from the wrath to come. While this is transpiring on earth, John has to be transferred to heaven to view the great scene of our Lord receiving His Kingdom at the hands of the Father. This transfer of John may have been similar to the experience of Paul in 2 Corinthians 12:2-4. "I knew a man in Christ above fourteen years ago, (whether in the body, I cannot tell; or whether out of the body, I cannot tell: God knoweth;) such an one caught up to the third heaven. And I knew such a man, (whether in the body or out of the body, I cannot tell: God knoweth;) How that he was caught up into paradise, and heard unspeakable words, which it is not lawful for a man to utter."

We also wonder what happened to the many bodies which came out of the graves after the resurrection of Jesus? Matthew 27:52-53: "And the graves were opened; and many bodies of the saints which slept arose, and came out of the graves after his resurrection, and went into the holy city, and appeared unto many." Did they go back into their graves or did Jesus take them to paradise as the "first-fruit?" We personally adhere to the latter for we read in Ephesians 4:8, "Wherefore he saith, when he ascended up on high, he led captivity captive, and gave gifts unto men." And one must consider all the saved *souls* and *spirits* not yet given resurrected bodies. Hebrews 12:23 says: "But ye are come to the general assembly and church of the first-born, which are written to heaven, and to God the judge of all, and to the spirits of just men made perfect." And Revelation 6:9b says: "I saw under the altar the souls of them that were slain for the word of God."

Night Visions

Daniel saw the same glorious sight. Daniel 7:22 says: "Until the Ancient of days came, and judgment was given to the saints of the most High." The Ancient of days was enthroned and "One" like unto a "Son of Man" brought near before Him and given "dominion and glory and a kingdom, that all the peoples, and languages should serve Him." Daniel was not invited to heaven, but saw all in "night visions." There was no "come up hither." The reason for this was that Daniel was *not* of the Church but he was God's earthly people, Israel, and was not taken up to heaven. John, however, belonging to the Church, heard "come up hither, and I will show thee." The voice as it were a trumpet, was not an angel trumpet, but the voice of Christ to show what would occur *after* the church-age.

How Far is Heaven?

Verse two shows us the "heavenly throne." The Holy Spirit opened his eyes to see. How far is heaven? Just the opening of eyes. In 2 Kings 6:17 we read: "And Elisha prayed, and said, Lord, I pray thee, open his eyes, that he may see. And the Lord opened the eyes of the young man; and he saw: and, behold, the mountain was full of horses and chariots of fire round about Elisha." Here we see the king of Syria warring against Israel. Syria got nowhere since the prophet Elisha told the king of Israel where the enemy was. In the end, the king of Syria compassed the city where Elisha was. When Elisha's servant saw the army, he was afraid and told Elisha of his fear of the enemy. Then Elisha prayed, "Lord, open his eyes," and he saw horses and chariots of fire on the mountain. The heavenly host was just the "opening of eyes" away. The throne in heaven introduced the prophetic part of the revelation.

A Throne Set

In verse two, the "throne set" was not "in sight during the first three chapters. Nor was it seen by Adam, nor Abraham or the patriarchs, for they were *walking by faith* and building altars for worship. The ark of covenant was a type of the throne on high. The throne of *grace* today will become the throne of judgment later on.

Let us note some particulars about that throne:

A. It is the throne of the Triune Eternal God, set in heaven and surrounded by a rainbow.

B. Around the throne are twenty-four elders according to verse four. These are crowned and on thrones about the throne of God. They must be representatives of mankind for angels are not crowned nor do they sit on thrones. Angels are ministering servants. Hebrews 1:14 says: "Are they not all ministering spirits, sent forth to minister for them who shall be heirs of salvation?" The throne here could well be a symbol of the judgment seat of Christ (2 Cor. 5:10). Crowns and thrones are promised to redeemed men. Revelation 2:10b says: "Be thou faithful unto death, and I will give thee a crown of life."

C. There were lightnings and voices and thunders (vs. 5). These were powers of nature to be intelligible to man and they refer to judgment. 1 Corinthians 6:2-3 says: "Do ye not know that the saints shall judge the world? Know ye not that we shall judge angels?"

D. There were seven lamps of fire and they represent the seven spirits of God. Verse five shows the Holy Spirit in fullness.

E. There is also the glassy sea before the throne (vs. 6). It seemed to John as such. It portrays the holiness of God and in holiness God acknowledges *four* companies of redeemed men.

The Redeemed

1. Old Testament saints. Hebrews 12:1a: "Wherefore seeing we also are compassed about with so great a cloud of witnesses."

2. New Testament saints of the church. Ephesians 5:27a: "That he might present it to himself a glorious church."

3. The 144,000 Jews – a distinct company. Revelation 7:4b: "...and there were sealed an hundred and forty and four thousand of all the tribes of the children of Israel."

4. The great multitude of tribulation saints. Revelation 7:9: "After this I beheld, and, lo, a great multitude, which no man could number, of all nations, and kindreds, and people, and tongues, stood before the throne, and before the Lamb, clothed with white robes, and palms in their hands." These are a separate company from the Church and Old Testament saints.

Cherubim

The four living creatures adhere to the Greek name "Zoa" and denote "living ones," being active and praising God always. The idea expressed is that these creatures have their activity imparted to them divinely by God. It denotes divine life. They are described in verses seven and eight. They are cherubim who support the throne. They are aware of God's ways. Cherubim have to do with protecting the holy acts of God. Genesis 3:24 says: "So he drove out the man; and he placed at the east of the garden of Eden Cherubims, and a flaming sword which turned every way, to keep the way of the tree of life." Another class – Seraphim – deals with uncleanness in man. Isaiah 6:6-7 says: "Then flew one of the Seraphims unto me, having a live coal in his hand, which he had taken with the tongs from off the altar: And he laid it upon my mouth, and said, Lo, this hath touched thy lips; and thine iniquity is taken away, and thy sin purged." The four "beasts" represent whatever is noblest, strongest, wisest and swiftest in nature. Created life has implanted desire to worship the Uncreated – the one who liveth forever and ever.

Victory

In verse ten, the twenty-four elders cast their crowns before the throne. These crowns are not "diadema" crowns or even "monarch's" crowns, but they are "victor's crowns," called in the Greek *stephanos*. They have obtained them through victory over sin.

Seven Acts

Then, in verse eleven, God's creatorship is shown. Creation is for His pleasure, not in a sinful sense but in a holy, sincere and just sense. Here we note seven acts of the twenty-four elders. We see these elders in Revelation 21:12,14: "And had a wall great and high, and had twelve gates, and at the gates twelve angels, and names written thereon, which are the names of the twelve tribes of the children of Israel: And the wall of the city had twelve foundations, and in them the names of the twelve apostles of the Lamb."

1. They sit on thrones (Rev. 4:4).
2. They worship God (Rev. 4:9-11).
3. They cast their crowns before God (Rev. 4:10).
4. They fall prostrate before God (Rev. 4:10).
5. They sing and play harps (Rev. 5:8,10).
6. They act as priests (Rev. 5:8).
7. They give John the revelation of the Lamb slain (Rev. 5:5).

A Reason for Creation

Verse eleven of chapter four shows why God should receive glory and honour and power. Colossians 1:16 says: "For by Him were all things created, that are in heaven, and that are on earth, visible and invisible, whether they be thrones, or dominions, or principalities, or powers: all things were created by him, and for him." And 1 Corinthians 8:6 says: "But to us there is but one God, the Father, of whom are all things, and we in him; and one Lord Jesus Christ, by whom are all things, and we by him." He is given glory and honour and power because He has brought into being all that exists. And all was created because of His will. This contradicts the theory of evolution, which is only a theory. Someone has summed it all up in these words: "Men believe that there is a God, not because they can prove His existence by scientific demonstration, but because there is no other answer to their ultimate questions and deepest needs." "Our minds and all our experience compel us to believe that for every effect there must be an adequate cause," someone else has said.

The Seven-Sealed Book

The Key

Chapters four and five are as one and contain the key to the rest of Revelation. Verses one to four show us the "heavenly Book." Let us note some facts in chapter five.

The Seven Seals

1. First of all, we have the seven-sealed book, fully written and ready to be opened. It is closed and sealed, indicating finality and privacy. A good example is given in Ruth 4:1-12. When a man lost his possession to another, he was brought before the elders and it was established before them. When the year of jubilee (50 years) came, the possession must be returned to the first owner. It could be bought back in the meantime (before the end of 50 years) in two ways. One, he could buy it back or two, a kinsman could buy it, if he did not buy it, as Boaz did. Two papers were prepared. The kinsman could read the unsealed paper and then pay and ask for the sealed paper. This is our

picture here. Christ redeemed us and now asks for and opens the sealed book for the redemption of all nature, for all belongs to Him and not to Satan.

Gabriel

2. All creation could not look upon the book nor open it, and the angel asked, "Who is worthy to open the book (Greek: scroll) and to loosen the seals of it?" Gabriel, the angel, seems to be employed in the chief service. Daniel 9:21-22 shows how Gabriel was used to bring the message to men. "Yea, whiles I was speaking in prayer, even the man Gabriel, whom I had seen in the vision at the beginning, being caused to fly swiftly, touched me about the time of the evening oblation. And he informed me... and said, O Daniel, I am now come forth to give thee skill and understanding." Another angel, Michael, has to do with Israel. Daniel 10:13 says: "But the prince of the kingdom of Persia withstood me one and twenty days: but, lo, Michael, one of the chief princes, came to help me." John is sorrowful at the delay of God's longed for Kingdom. He wept much because no one could be found to open the scroll and look at it. Then one of the elders pointed him to the heavenly Lamb who, as the "lion of the tribe of Judah, prevailed to open the seals." The Lamb appeared to have been slain, but was in the midst of the elders. We must note here that the "Lamb slain" was in retrospect as in chapter twelve. It had happened some time before, that Jesus had been slain, but it was now mentioned as if it were happening now. The "slain Lamb" is such *for all time.* That is why, in verse six, it says: "as it had been slain." Here see also

the Lamb with the seven spirits who know all earth's affairs.

The Lamb Opens the Seals

The Lamb took the book from the hand of God. It is the taking of governmental power by the Mediator which is the burden of the Old Testament prophecy and creation (vs. 7-8). Here, then, is the worship of the Lamb, in verses eight to twelve. Worship to the Lamb is now founded not merely upon creation but also upon redemption, for we read, "Thou wast slain." And this becomes the "universal worship" of beasts and elders, to God and the Lamb. Verse nine can be true only of the redeemed.

The Lord As the Slain Lamb

Let us now restate the main points. In the first chapter we see Christ as "Lord." Now He is seen as "the slain Lamb," but invested with an exalted position. All events have been bent toward one event, "the investiture of Jesus." And He is the slain Lamb who cannot compromise with the iniquity the world loves. And we, as His followers, need to beware of being found to be handling the worldly goods. And in verse eight we hear that the "prayers" of the saints had something to do with this event. The Lord had instructed His disciples to say, "Thy kingdom come; Thy will be done, as in heaven, so on earth." How important our prayers are.

John is Weeping

John wept when no one was found to open the book (vs. 4). It seemed as if sin and Satan were to go on forever in control of the affairs of this world. We, too, need to vex our righteous souls, as Lot did, as we see their lawless deeds.

A New Song

Then look at the *new* song (vs. 9). It is up to date and more. But it is still about the slain Lamb and redemption. Nothing is more contemporary or modern. It is real and true worship. The blood of Christ as the price of our redemption runs all through the Revelation. It is Love's Final Solution for all mankind. "For every kindred, and tongue, and people, and nation."

A Kingdom and Priests

Verse nine needs repetition. "And they sing a new song, saying: Worthy art thou to receive the scroll and to open the seals of it, because thou wast slain and didst purchase to God by the blood of thee out of every tribe and tongue and people and nation." And verse ten says: "And didst make *them* (Greek: *autous*) to the God of us a kingdom and priests and they will reign on the earth." It is a prophetic use anticipating the final result.

Angels

At last the angels are admitted into the circle (where the Church has been) of worshippers. In verses eleven and twelve, we see Hebrews 1:6 fulfilled and the angels' desire also fulfilled. 1 Peter 1:12 says: "Unto whom it was revealed, that not unto themselves, but unto us they did minister the things, which are now reported unto you by them that have preached the gospel unto you with the Holy Ghost sent down from heaven; which things the angels desire to look into."

Numerous and Numberless

Look at the number of angels: one hundred million and then some. And they knew all along that Jesus was the Son of God even when men crucified Him. And now they say: "Worthy is the Lamb." It has tremendous meaning. Here is the number *seven* again – power, riches, wisdom, strength, honour, glory and blessing, all belong to Jesus. This universal chorus of praise to Christ from all created life reminds one of the deep mystical passage in Romans 8:20-22. "For the creature was made subject to vanity, not willingly, but by reason of him who hath subjected the same in hope, because the creature itself also shall be delivered from the bondage of corruption into the glorious liberty of the children of God. For we know that the whole creation groaneth and travaileth in pain together until now."

Confession

When all of this occurs, where will the mockers be, and the infidels and modernistic preachers and professors? No creature will be omitted. Every knee shall bow and every tongue confess that He is Lord.

The Authority of Jesus

It requires lawful authority to break a seal. Jesus is that authority. As He breaks each seal, there will be a separate special revelation of His purpose.

The Seventieth Week

In this connection we need to read Daniel 9:24-27, dealing with the seventieth week and applying it to Israel, for it shows Israel's (Jacob's Trouble) in the tribulation of Revelation 6:1 and 19:21. Here then is Daniel 9:24-27.

"Seventy weeks are determined upon thy people and upon thy holy city, to finish the transgression, and to make an end of sins, and to make reconciliation for iniquity, and to bring in everlasting righteousness, and to seal up the vision and prophecy, and to anoint the most Holy. Know therefore and understand, that from the going forth of the commandment to restore and to build Jerusalem unto the Messiah the Prince shall be seven weeks, and threescore and two weeks: the street shall be built again, and the wall, even in troublous time. And after threescore and two weeks shall Messiah be cut off, but not for himself: and the people of the prince that shall come shall destroy the city and the sanctuary: and the end thereof shall be with a flood, and unto the end of the war desolations are determined. And he shall confirm the covenant with many for one week: and in the midst of the week he shall cause the sacrifice and the oblation to cease, and for the overspreading of abominations he shall make it desolate, even until the consummation, and that determined shall be poured upon the desolate."

A Six-fold Purpose

These seventy weeks have to do with the Jews and Jerusalem, and have a six-fold purpose:

1. To finish the Transgression (of Israel) which will end when, as a nation, they will be converted.

2. To make an end of sin (sins of Israel).

3. To make reconciliation for iniquity (rejection of Messiah).

4. To bring in everlasting righteousness (millennium).

5. To seal up the vision and prophecy (no more need of vision or prophet).

6. To anoint the most holy (temple in millennium).

The seventy weeks are divided into three periods: of seven weeks, sixty-two weeks, and one week. They cover the time from the going forth of the commandment to restore and to build Jerusalem, 445 B.C., to the second coming of Christ. The seven weeks refer to the time required to build the walls of Jerusalem (49 years). The sixty-two and seven weeks (making 69 weeks) deal with restoring Jerusalem to the Messiah the Prince (Jesus).

A Number of Years

New then: 7 x 69 = 483 years. Also using the calender years of 360 days: 483 x 360 = 173,880 days. Beginning with 445 B.C., it would take us to the crucifixion. Now there is a time lapse of almost two thousand years until the seventieth week begins. Chapter five ends with silent adoration that closes the whole service of praise to the One upon the throne and to the Lamb. Here the representatives of the redeemed bow in silent worship. It is the worship by the universe. Philippians 2:10 says: "That at the name of Jesus every knee should bow; of things in heaven, and things in earth, and things under the earth." And verse eleven says: "And that every tongue should confess that Jesus Christ is Lord, to the glory of God the Father."

REVELATION 6

The Seven Seals

The Antichrist and His Opponent

In Revelation 6 we begin to deal with Daniel's seventieth week and the tribulation in its first three and a half years. Here, then, is the rise of the antichrist. In Daniel 9:27, the prince (antichrist) will confirm the covenant at the *beginning* of the week. But before the antichrist appears, the one in 2 Thessalonians 2:7 (the restraining One) must be taken out of the way. Therefore, if the antichrist appears at the beginning of the week, and the "One" in 2 Thessalonians 2:7 must first be taken out of the way, then it follows that the "One" is taken out of the way also at the beginning of the week. And the "One" being the Holy Spirit who lives in the true Church will mean that the Church will be taken out of the way also at the beginning of the seventieth week of tribulation.

The Seals

We must now consider the seals of chapter six. They cover the whole book of the new creation, for the seventh seal contains the seven trumpets and the seventh trumpet sounds forth the seven vials of wrath of God, of Revelation 16 which reveals the revelation of judgments preceding the Lord's second coming. Revelation 17 and 18 are a detailed description of the judgment of Babylon the Great (Rev. 16:19).

The Opening of the Seals

Let us remember that the *Lamb opens* all the seals while still in heaven, and He cannot be the rider on the white horse. The four living beings have to do directly with the first four seals. They know God's will and purpose and carry it out. The word "come" is addressed to the four horsemen, not to John. "And see" is not in the Greek Testament.

The First Seal

The first seal in verse two shows the horse and rider. Some believe the horse and rider are related to "the holy hosts and armies that are in heaven." But since this comes after the sixty-nine weeks of Daniel and begins the seventieth week of Daniel, we believe it is the antichrist that is spoken of here. Daniel 9 shows him going forth as a prince and making a covenant with the world and Israel (Dan. 9:26-27). The world is waiting for such a man.

In verse two we note that "a crown was given him." Likely, it was given by one of the four living creatures under the permissive will of God. It was not a crown (*diadem*) of a peace loving monarch, but the crown (*stephanos*) of a warring victor. He has, however, a bow but no arrows. He must try to carry out his intentions through peace treaties. It is tempting to identify this rider with the Rider on the white horse in Revelation 19:11, whose name is "the word of God," but the two riders have nothing in common beyond the white horse.

The Second Seal

In the second seal, verse three, we have a rider on a red horse who takes peace from the earth. We seem to see the shadows of such action even today. We have distrust, plotting and killing all over the globe. The "restraining One" of 2 Thessalonians 2 is holding back human ulterior passions, but there will come a time when the murderous evil passions will be unleashed. Red means blood and a sword means war.

The Third Seal

The third seal brings famine. War brings bloodshed but also famine and hunger. During the Russian revolution in 1917-1919 many people died of starvation. The red colour turned to black as hunger gnawed away at bodily structure until a human being turned into a spectre or ghostlike apparition. The horse is black. The rider has a pair of balances in his hand. The expression "a penny" means a quart of wheat for a day's wage. It is a desperate situation. People waste away. No value is set on human life. No hurt shall come to oil and wine. More importance is attached to material things than human life. Oil is the bartering agent of the day. And there will be self-indulgence of the rich in those days. We have a foreshadowing of such a situation even in our day. Just how and on what are Christians spending their money? Someone has said: "By modern methods of agriculture we have solved the question of famine." That, however, is not a correct statement. Just let the Lord withhold the rain, or send too much during harvest and we face famine. This has happened in such a country as Ethiopia. But famine shall be much more severe during this time of which Revelation 6 speaks.

The Fourth Seal

The fourth seal is death in verses seven and eight. The horse is pale. Perhaps a greenish yellow or variegated as is described in Zechariah 6:3b: "and in the fourth chariot grisled and bay horses." Or perhaps an ashen colour of a face blanched by fear. Death is here spoken of as if he were a person. We would rather say it is a state, but death may be more than a state. It may be a terrible seizure or a keeper. Death could not hold Jesus as He was without sin. Death's inseparable companion is hades. In Revelation 1:18, hades is the abode of the dead, the keys of which Christ holds. The four scourges of Ezekiel 14:21 are here reproduced. "For thus saith the Lord God: How much more when I send my four sore judgments upon Jerusalem, the sword, and the famine, and the noisome beast, and the pestilence, to cut off from it man and beast." In Revelation 20:13, death and hades give up the dead which were in them. Death was holding the body and hades the spirit. Finally, death and hades are cast into the lake of fire. Whatever that power is that holds the bodies, it will be cast into the lake of fire and lose its power.

Death and Hell

To repeat, under the fourth seal we see death and hades given authority over the fourth part of the earth to kill with the sword, hunger, famine and the beasts. Prosperity will be changed into famine and hunger and pestilence which cannot be overcome. These plagues are by the permissive will of God and no one can withstand them. Hell is harvesting.

A Remnant

The fifth seal in verses nine to eleven deals with the martyred remnant. To Moses was given a pattern of the things in heaven. Hebrews 9:23 says: "It was therefore necessary that the patterns of things in the heavens should be purified with these; but the heavenly things themselves with better sacrifices than these." There is an altar there. To this place Jesus came to present Himself as the Great High Priest. Hebrews 9:12 says: "Neither by the blood of goats and calves, but by his own blood he entered in once into the holy place, having obtained eternal redemption for us."

Disembodied Souls

Under the altar in heaven are the souls (yet disembodied) of God's martyrs. Their martyrdom has cried to heaven as the blood of Abel cried for vengeance and justification. These souls show the change from grace to judgment. God delays the judgment, not for salvation, but that the rest of the martyrs may join their fellows.

A Fourth Dimension

Let us consider the soul for a moment. There are three dimensions, as we know them: length, breadth and depth. Einstein, the mathematician, spoke of a fourth dimension. Jesus, in His resurrection, shows the possibility of a fourth dimension. He ascended, which is still impossible for man, because man is burdened with a body of mortal flesh. The ascended body of Christ was not a spirit (ghost), nor a transfigured body (as on the mount of transfiguration), but a *changed* body. It could eat, go through unopened doors and be seen and felt. 1 Corinthians 15:51-53 says:

A Mystery

"Behold, I show you a mystery; we shall not all sleep, but we shall all be *changed*. In a moment, in the twinkling of an eye, at the last trump; for the trumpet shall sound, and the dead shall be raised incorruptible, and we shall be *changed*. For this corruptible must put on incorruption, and this mortal must put on immortality."

A Spirit Body

The soul is not the body, as some claim. The soul is that spirit body with which the spirit is clad (clothed). Luke 24:37-39 says: "But they were terrified and affrighted, and supposed that they had seen a spirit. And He said unto them, Why are ye troubled? and why do thoughts arise in your hearts? Behold my hands and my feet, that it is I myself; handle me, and see; for a spirit hath *not flesh* and *bones* as ye see me have." In 1 Kings 17:21-22 we read: "And he stretched himself upon the child three times, and cried unto the Lord, and said, O Lord my God, I pray thee, let this child's soul come into him again. And the Lord heard the voice of Elijah; and the soul of the child came into him again, and he revived."

The Character of a Soul

We see here where Elijah raises the widow's son who had died. He prayed the Lord to "let the child's *soul* come into him again. And the soul of the child came into him again." And now, under the altar, are the souls of those who had been martyred on the earth. We have other Scriptures that deal with the soul. Psalm 16:10 says: "Thou wilt not leave my soul in hell (sheol)." Psalm 107:9 speaks of a "hungry soul." Jeremiah 31:24 speaks of a "weary soul." Psalm 42:2 speaks of a "thirsty soul." Job 30:25 speaks of a "grieved soul." The soul is related to the body make-up as "body, soul and spirit" – a triunity, or trinity, similar to the Trinity of God. 1 Thessalonians 5:23 says: "And the very God of peace sanctify you wholly: and I pray God your whole spirit, and soul, and body, be preserved blameless unto the coming of our Lord Jesus Christ." The soul is the "self" person and, here in Revelation, disembodied. The soul indicates "self-consciousness," while the body indicates "world-consciousness" and the spirit indicates "God-consciousness." All of this shows that the spirit is the outbreathing or likeness of God's character in man, while the soul is the distinguishing mark of one person from another and from animals. Here are the distinguishing words or expressions in both Old and New Testaments.

Distinctions

Old Testament	New Testament
Hebrew	*Greek*
Body – Guyphah	Body – Soma
Flesh – Basar	Flesh – Sarx
Soul – Nephesh	Soul – Psuche
Spirit – Ruwach	Spirit – Pneuma

Souls Clad

The souls in Revelation 6:9-11 are given white robes (righteousness) and are to rest from their cry of vengeance and also rest in peace until their fellow-servants and their brethren should be slain. We must note here that souls can wear spiritual robes. The fifth seal exhibits three things:

Exhibits

1. The patience of God. He proceeds slowly and reluctantly from the dispensation of mercy and grace to that of judgment. 2 Peter 3:9 says: "The Lord is not slack concerning His promise, as some men count slackness; but is longsuffering to usward, not willing that any should perish, but that all should come to repentance." If only mankind could imitate God in this respect.

2. The change of dispensation in the prayers of these martyrs for vengeance. They are asking for judgment.

3. The utter wickedness of the earth. The dwellers on earth continue to martyr the full number of God's servants and saints. The world has no patience with godly people. The slaying continues between the "catching up" (rapture) and the opening of the sixth seal and onward. It continues even in the beginning of the seventieth week, while the cry goes up, "Peace, peace."

The Sixth Seal

In the opening of or breaking of the sixth seal we note the wrath of God beginning and ending with the trumpets and vials and Armageddon. Regarding the earthquake, these are on the increase today. But this one in Revelation will be a severe one for God is shaking the earth for or because of man's sin. This happened at both His crucifixion and resurrection. Matthew 27:51 and 28:2 speak of this: "And, behold, the veil of the temple was rent in twain from the top to the bottom; and the earth did quake and the rocks rent." "And, behold, there was a great earthquake; for the angel of the Lord descended from heaven, and came and rolled back the stone from the door, and sat upon it."

Sun and Moon Affected

Here we have the first darkening of the sun and moon before the terrible day of the Lord. The second darkening will be "immediately after the tribulation." Matthew 24:29 says: "Immediately after the tribulation of those days shall the sun be darkened, and the moon shall not give her light, and the stars shall fall from heaven, and the powers of the heavens shall be shaken."

Men believe that the end has come; when it does not, they harden their hearts as Pharaoh did, and in Revelation 19:19 they boldly gather against the Lamb whom here they dread (vs. 15). Here are various groups represented: chief captains, mighty men, rich men, bondmen and free men.

Joel 2:31 says: "The sun shall be turned into darkness, and the moon into blood, before the great and the terrible day of the Lord come." And Peter, interpreting Joel in Acts 2:20, says: "The sun shall be turned into darkness, and the moon into blood, before that great and notable day of the Lord come." Peter points the events to Pentecost and its events, but also to the Lord's Day and its events.

The Cry

There in unlimited terror upon all the earth. The throne seems to be seen by all those on the earth. They cry unto the mountains and rocks "fall on us and hide us" (vs. 16). In all of this men harden themselves and refuse repentance. They must face the great day of His wrath and such cannot be the Church as some maintain. Sinners dread not so much death as the Presence of Christ.

Meanwhile, God gives us, in chapter seven, a vision of His election and salvation – Love's Final Solution.

The Sealed Israelites

The Trumpet Judgments

In chapter seven we have a parenthetical passage. It is inserted between the sixth and seventh seals and explains what will transpire from the sixth seal to the rest of the week. Here we stand before the great trumpet judgments.

We have here three section:

A. The staying of the four angels from "harming" the earth (vs. 3).

B. The sealing of the 144,000 of the remnant of Israel, who will go through the great time of trouble. They need to be marked just as the seven thousand of Elijah and Ahab's time were remembered who were left as a remnant (vs. 4-8).

C. The great victorious multitude, who, in tribulation, are martyred and in whose number are included the saints under the altar (vs. 9-11).

The Sealing

The above sealing is not like the sealing done in Ephesians 1:13-14. Here we read: "In whom ye also trusted, after that ye heard the word of truth, the gospel of your salvation: in whom also after that ye believed, ye were sealed with the Holy Spirit of promise. Which is the earnest of our inheritance until the redemption of the purchased possession, unto the praise of his glory."

In Ephesians the Holy Spirit is Himself the seal, after they have been saved. The seal here in Ephesians denotes:

A. *A finished transaction.* Jeremiah 32:9-10 reads: "And I bought the field of Hanameel my uncle's son, that was in Anathoth, and weighed him the money, even seventeen shekels of silver. And I subscribed the evidence, and sealed it, and took witnesses, and weighed him the money in the balances."

B. *Ownership.* Jeremiah 32:11-12 says: "So I took the evidence of the purchase, both that which was sealed according to the law and custom, and that which was open: and I gave the evidence of the purchase unto Baruch... and in the presence of the witnesses that subscribed the book of the purchase, before all the Jews that sat in the court of the prison."

C. *Security.* Esther 8:8 says: "Write ye also for the Jews, as it liketh you, in the king's name and seal it with the king's ring: for the writing which is written in the king's name, and sealed with the king's ring, may no man reverse."

Another Seal

But the seal here in Revelation 6 is of angels. Angels have a great part in the tribulation period. They seal those who believe in God during this troubled time. Chapters 8-16 show us the trouble through which the sealed ones pass.

These 144,000 are the remnant of the remnant of Israel on earth at that time – twelve thousand from each tribe. The tribes of Dan and Ephraim are left out because they had introduced idolatry. 1 Kings 12:25-30 says: "Then Jeroboam, built Shechem in Mount Ephraim, and dwelt therein; and went out from thence, and built Penuel. And Jeroboam said in his heart, now shall the kingdom return to the house of David; If this people go up to do sacrifice in the house of the Lord at Jerusalem, then shall the heart of this people turn again unto their lord, even unto Rehoboam king of Judah, and they shall kill me, and go again to Rehoboam king of Judah. Whereupon the king took counsel, and made two calves of gold and said unto them, it is too much for you to go up to Jerusalem; behold thy gods, O Israel, which brought thee up out of the land of Egypt. And set the one in Bethel, and the other put he in Dan. And this thing became a sin."

Reinstated

However, Ezekiel 48 shows them reinstated in the millennium. These two tribes must, apparently, go through the tribulation unsealed. Such is the divine justice of God. It is Love's Final Solution, even for the disobedient who repent. These 144,000 are that remnant of a remnant of Israel which meet the Lord when He comes at His second coming. Zechariah 13:9 says: "And I will bring the third part through the fire and will refine them as silver is refined, and will try them as gold is tried; they shall call on my name, and I will hear them; I will say, it is my people: and they shall say, the Lord is my God." And Malachi 3:17 says: "And they shall be mine, saith the Lord of hosts, in that day when I make up my jewels, and I will spare them, as a man spareth his own son that serveth him."

Not Too Small

Some object and say the number is too small. But God said: "If the number of Israel be as the sand of the sea, it is the remnant that shall be saved" (Isa. 10:22). Much of the nation will perish under the blows of the last enemy of God. Zechariah 14:1-3 says: "Behold, the day of the Lord cometh, and thy spoil shall be divided in the midst of thee. For I will gather all nations against Jerusalem to battle; and the city shall be taken, and the houses rifled, and the women ravished: and half of the city shall go forth into captivity, and the residue of the people shall not be cut off from the city. Then shall the Lord go forth, and fight against those nations, as when he fought in the day of battle."

The Rod

And Ezekiel 20:36-38 says: "Like as I pleaded with your fathers in the wilderness of the land of

Egypt, *so will I plead with you*, saith the Lord God. And I will cause you to pass under the rod, and I will bring you into the bond of the covenant: And I will purge out from among you the rebels, and them that transgress against me: I will bring them forth out of the country where they sojourn, and they shall not enter into the land of Israel: and ye shall know that I am the Lord."

Israel

The nation of Israel is gathered back to Israel or Palestine for the coming trouble. Leaders of socialism, atheism and godless commercialism are found among the Jewish people. They are gathered back in unbelief, trusting their money and ability to survive. But God has 144,000 faithful ones.

A Great Multitude

Not only the 144,000 elect remnant of Israel are found here, but also a great multitude, which no man could number, out of every nation and of all tribes and people and tongues, will have their place "before the throne of heaven."

Note Matthew 25:31-32: "When the Son of man shall come in his glory, and all the holy angels with him, then shall he sit upon the throne of his glory: And before him shall be gathered all nations; and he shall separate them one from another, as a shepherd divideth his sheep from the goats."

Gentiles

This Scripture shows those Gentiles who go into the millennium with the 144,000 in their natural bodies, but are not this great multitude here.

Unknown

John does not know who they are. He would have known the Old Testament saints since he and Peter and James knew Moses and Elijah on the mount of transfiguration. Also he would have known the church saints. He is told that they "come out of the great tribulation," "And have washed their robes, and made them white in the blood of the Lamb." They are not of Christ's body, the Church, but saved.

The Gospel of the Kingdom

This great multitude must come out of the Gentile nations and are saved during the great tribulation. We do not find that they reign with Christ a thousand years. They form a different group from Israel's remnant and the Church. They are before God and are in the temple. (Gentiles cannot serve in Jewish temples on earth.) They are not angels, for the angels are glad for them (vs. 11). To these was preached the Gospel of the Kingdom. The white robes are signs of victory and joy.

Surprised

We shall be happily surprised as to who is saved in those terrible days of the tribulation. Jesus said, "In my Father's house are many mansions, I go to prepare a place for you." Other saved companies, aside from the Church, shall be there. Those who have been in touch with one or another of God's children and have discussed the rapture and the tribulation shall remember the discussion, and shall be saved during the tribulation. Suffer, yes, but in the fold. The great tribulation is not only wrath upon the ungodly, but also a time of salvation for others. It is, as Revelation 3:10 says, the "hour of trial." And, according to verse fourteen, "These are they which came out of great tribulation, and have washed their robes, and made them white in the blood of the Lamb." There is no power in the blood of the martyrs to cleanse from sin, but alone in the blood of the Lamb. The result is "white" not "red" as one might imagine. And there is sacred fellowship here, as verse fifteen tells us. And God's Presence is their protection from all the weaknesses of the human body (vs. 16). Human appetites will be gone. These are "before the throne of God, and serve Him day and night in His temple." And He on the throne shall dwell among them. The Lamb shall feed them and lead them to the living fountains of water. "And God shall wipe away all tears from their eyes." The psalmist, David, expresses this thought so wonderfully in Psalm 23. It bears repetition:

"The Lord is my Shepherd; I shall not want. He maketh me to lie down in green pastures: He leadeth me beside the still waters, He restoreth my soul: He leadeth me in the paths of righteousness for his name's sake, Yea, though I walk through the valley of the shadow of death, I will fear no evil; for thou art with me; thy rod and thy staff they comfort me. Thou preparest a table before me in the presence of mine enemies: thou anointest my head with oil: my cup runneth over. Surely goodness and mercy shall follow me all the days

of my life: and I will dwell in the house of the Lord for ever."

What a wonderful Saviour we have – who loves even in the tribulation. Therefore we refer again to the title of this book, Love's Final Solution.

REVELATION 8

The Four Trumpet Judgments

The Seventh Seal

When the Lamb opens the seventh seal of the Book of judgment, there is silence in heaven for about half an hour. No elder or angel speaks, no chorus of praise nor cry of adoration, no thunder from the throne, is heard. All worship ends and there is no creative activity. Why? It would seem that the steps of God, from mercy to judgment, are always slow, reluctant and measured. In chapter six men slay one another. The fourth seal sets forth death by sword, famine, pestilence and wild beasts. But these cannot be compared to such judgment as under the trumpets. There is silence. God has no pleasure in the death of the ones who die without a Saviour. He is love and here is Love's Final Solution.

Silence

This is the calm before the storm. Imagine it. God, the Lamb, the four living beings, the twenty-four elders, the seraphim, the millions of angels, the Church, the martyrs beneath the altar, all silent. That is the problem of sin and judgment before God. And man takes all this sin question so lightly.

Seven Angels With Trumpets

Seven angels stood before God in verse two. Someone has named them: Uriel, Raphael, Raguel, Michael, Sariel, Gabriel and Remiel. And what a scene it was. The angels were each given a trumpet. In Israel the trumpet sound was used for calling the princes and congregation together. Another sounding was for journeying and as an alarm to warn against the enemy (Num. 10:1-6). The alarm here is for the earth dwellers (vs 5). In like manner, the trumpet sounding was against Jericho in the time of Joshua. Joshua 6:13 says: "And seven priests, bearing seven trumpets of ram's horns before the ark of the Lord went on continually, and blew with the trumpets: and the armed men went before them; but the rearward came after the ark of the Lord, the priests going on, and blowing with the trumpets." And Joel 2:1 says: "Blow ye the trumpet in Zion, and sound an alarm in my holy mountain: let all the inhabitants of the land tremble: for the day of the Lord cometh, for it is nigh at hand."

Three Things

The angel that had the incense in the censer (vessel) was not Christ. Christ is the Lamb opening the seals. This angel brings before all heaven three things:

1. The prayers of all the saints (vs. 4). No saint's prayer is ever forgotten.

2. The incense refers to the Lord's person and work at Calvary and makes the prayers of the saints effectual before God. One hardly realizes the importance of fervent prayers.

3. These prayers, on behalf of Christ's atonement, bring about the judgment. It is the answer, at last, to the prayer "Thy Kingdom come." Now begins God's hour of intervention regarding sin and the cause of sin.

A Reversal

Even the order of the elements is reversed here. We know that first is the lightning, then thunder. But here first of all is thunder, then lightning, then the earthquake (vs. 5).

Trumpet Judgments

Now, behold four of the seven trumpet judgments. They are direct visitations from heaven upon men on earth. The first four trumpets are very much like the plagues in Egypt. They announce the plagues to come. The first trumpet sounds and there is hail and fire mingled with blood (vs. 7). The third part of trees and grass are burnt up. Exodus 9:23 says: "And Moses stretched forth his rod toward heaven: and the Lord sent thunder and hail, and the fire ran along upon the ground." And we believe it is just as literal as in Egypt. This has not happened since then and is for the future, after the church age.

The Second Trumpet

The second trumpet brings and casts something like a great mountain, burning with fire, into the sea (vs. 8). The third part of the sea became blood. Just like Exodus 7:20b says: "And all the waters that were in the river were turned to blood." The Mediterranean sea is close by. And the third part of the creatures in the sea died (vs. 9). And the third part of the ships were destroyed. One third is God's number. It stands for a visitation or judgment of God.

The Third Trumpet

The third trumpet shows a great star (perhaps a meteor) falling upon the third part of the rivers and fountains of water (vs. 10). And many died by drinking these waters. They were mixed with wormwood (vs. 11). It is the bitterest shrub known. It is found in the east, in Syria and Palestine. To cut off the water supply is to render humanity desperate and helpless.

The Fourth Trumpet

In the fourth trumpet sound, a third part of the sun is darkened, and a third part of the moon and a third part of the stars. Light is life and it gives the seasons of the year. All of this will be changed. A third part of the day will be dark (vs. 12). The powers of heaven are shaken. Men's confidence has been in the fact that "all things continue as they were (in the Greek, "all things remain so as from the beginning of creation") in the fixity of nature's laws." Now all is changed. Man becomes confused and fearful. Israel's remnant will have to cry out as Psalm 46 says: "God is our refuge and strength, a very present help in trouble."

Woe, Woe, Woe

Then comes the voice of the angel (Greek: eagle, a symbol of vengeance) (vs. 13). And we hear the voice saying, "Woe, woe, woe to those living on earth." Trumpets five, six and seven will bring a new quality of disaster.

Time to Repent

During these days of tribulation, the Lamb, still opening the seals, is still available to such who repent and submit to His will. Tribulation, too, is Love's Final Solution for the sin question. The proof of such a statement is the tribulation saints of Revelation 20:4: "And I saw thrones, and they sat upon them, and judgment was given unto them: and I saw the souls of them that were beheaded for the witness of Jesus, and for the word of God, and which had not worshiped the beast, neither his image, neither had received his mark upon their foreheads, or in their hands: and they lived and reigned with Christ a thousand years."

The Fifth and Sixth Trumpets

Fifth Trumpet

We now have the sounding of the trumpets of the fifth and sixth angels and when the fifth angel sounded, a star fell from heaven to the earth and had given unto him the key of the shaft of the abyss. We must note that the star came out of heaven, the place of purity and holiness and he "was given" the key, which was, no doubt, given by an angel at the command of God.

The Heart of the Earth

That there is a passage from the earth to its heart is verified by Revelation 20:1-3, which reads: "And I saw an angel come down from heaven, having the key of the bottomless pit and a great chain in his hand. And he laid hold on the dragon, that old serpent, which is the devil and Satan, and bound him a thousand years. And cast him into the bottomless pit, and shut him up, and set a seal upon him, that he should deceive the nations no more, till the thousand years should be fulfilled; and after that he must be loosed a little season."

Satan himself is cast down there and the passage is sealed for one thousand years. It is called "abyss" in the Greek in the above-mentioned Scripture (meaning bottomless place).

The Abyss

This "abyss" (bottomless pit) is not hades (the place of the wicked departed), nor is it "Tartarus" (the place of the fallen angels). 2 Peter 2:4 says: "For if God spared not the angels that sinned, but cast them down to hell (*tartarus*), and delivered them into chains of darkness, to be reserved unto judgment." Nor is it "Gehenna" (the place of the fiery lake). It is the place of the evil spirits or demons. They seem not to be Satan's angels, rather they are disembodied evil spirits, perhaps of the pre-adamic earth and trying to embody themselves again in some bodies, as they do here.

Gadara

In Jesus' time (Luke 8:31), Jesus drove out the demons from the Gadara possessed man and He allowed them to pass into the swine and the swine ran into the sea. These locusts in verse three must be evil spirits... demons, led by the evil angel (king) of the abyss (vs. 11). The plague of demonic locusts is here turned loose. The Israelites were permitted to eat them, but when the swarms came like the eighth Egyptian plague (Exod. 10:1ff), they devoured every green thing. They seemed like a lobster that lurks in stone walls in warm regions, with a venomous sting in its tail. And as Israel in

Egypt escaped the plagues which punished their neighbours, so the new Israel is exempted from the attack of the locusts of the abyss. And their work is to plague those who are not sealed. The plague lasts five months (the span of life for locusts). We know that John the Baptist ate ordinary locusts. These are different. They are unclean. Here are eight proofs that they are not ordinary locusts:

Locusts

1. They eat no grass, vegetables or trees as ordinary ones do.

2. They have a king (vs. 11).

3. They are not stifled by the smoke or burned by the fire of the abyss (vs. 2-11).

4. They are confined to the infernal regions due to sin (vs. 1-11).

5. They are spirit beings and, therefore, indestructible by mortal man.

6. They are intelligent beings – taking commands (vs. 4-6).

7. They have power to torment men – ordinary ones have not that power.

8. Their description proves them to be intelligent spirit beings, but with:

   A. Bodies like horses (vs. 7).
   B. Heads like men.
   C. Crowns like gold (vs. 7).
   D. Hair like women (vs. 8).
   E. Teeth like lions (vs. 8).
   F. Breastplate of iron (vs. 9).

G. Wings (vs. 9).

H. Tails and a scorpion sting (vs. 9).

Seeking Death

In those days of trumpet sounding, men shall seek death and shall not find it (vs. 6). "Such a death as they desire, a death which will end their sufferings, is impossible; physical death is no remedy for the basanismos (torment) of an evil conscience" (Swete). "Paul in Philippians 1:23 shows a preference for death if his work is done, in order to be with Christ, a very different feeling from what we have here" (A.T. Robertson, Word Pictures in the New Testament). But these locusts cannot harm those who have the seal of God in their foreheads (vs. 4). Our bodies are mortal and are subject to death. But in those days of trouble death shall flee from men.

Abaddon

The word "Abaddon" means "destruction." The word "Apollyon" means "destroyer." Destruction has begun. It is like a terminal cancer, eating away unseen and unnoticed. Like sin that destroys unobserved. Suddenly there is pain but not death. Death must wait for another time.

No Annihilation

But destruction does not mean annihilation. Pilate was asked by the crowd to release Barabbas but to destroy (apollumi) Jesus. But we know that it was impossible to destroy Jesus. The word "destroy" could mean death or separation or punishment but not annihilation.

The Sixth Trumpet

Now we have the sixth angel sounding (vs. 13), and we see four angels that were bound, loosed. They had been prepared for this ordeal to kill the third part of men (vs. 15).

The Euphrates rises in Armenia and joins the Tigris in lower Babylonia, a length of nearly 1800 miles, the eastern boundary of the Roman Empire next to Parthia. Euphrates is the place where human sin began and it seems, the first murder committed. Also there the first war confederacy was made (Gen. 14). Nimrod began to be mighty and the vast system of Babylonian idolatry began here, with its trinity of evil, "father, mother and son" (The two Babylons, by Hislop). Here, also, iniquity is to have its last stage on earth. Zechariah 5:3a says: "Then said He unto me, this is the curse that goeth forth over the face of the whole earth."

Satan's Army vs. Michael's Army

Two hundred million horsemen (vs. 16) are not human beings. They are Satan's army. The devil has an army too. Revelation 12:7 says: "And there was war in heaven; Michael and his angels fought against the dragon; and the dragon fought and his angels." These bring fire and smoke and brimstone (sulphur). It was literal in Genesis 19:24 where it says: "Then the Lord rained upon Sodom and upon Gomorrah brimstone and fire from the Lord out of heaven," and so it is here.

No Repentance

God's reason for all of this is that men should repent and they did not repent. A third part of men are killed. The two-thirds of mankind still spared did not change their creed or their conduct. And what were their sins? Verse twenty names them as the works of their hands, that they should not worship what their hands had made – idols of gold and silver and brass and stone and wood. Could ornaments be included in that list? And could mankind worship all kinds of bearded facial expressions? It is rather surprising what our hands are able to accomplish and what trouble they can get us into. Verse twenty-one says that their consciences were seared but they did not repent because they loved sin – sorcery. fornication and thefts. The word for sorcery is *pharmakia* and means "the administering of drugs," or a desire for magical arts or visions which drugs provide. Fornication (illicit sexual intercourse) is closely associated with this. The word for "thief" is *klepto* – one who abuses his confidence for his own gain. Gain is the selfish motive here. These are the characteristics of demonic worship and idolatry.

Because of such sin, the earth's population is lessened before Christ establishes the thousand year reign. This occasion here is the time of the taste of death and hell on earth. Idolatry is practiced. And one wonders about all the charms being worn today and the charming of others by means of drugs. Even enchantments are used, which is the calling of the energies of the evil spirit-world into human affairs by whatever means.

Fornication

Another sin is fornication. One needs only to look at newspapers, magazines, advertisements and T.V. to see what a wave of lust has begun. We seem to have surpassed Sodom with its bent for homosexuality. Romans 1 speaks of this. The world seems to live for self-indulgence in sexual relations. And such a trend has even invaded Christian circles.

Riches

The final sin is to "get money" by whatever means. Dishonesty, trickery, is the law of the day. One needs only to use cheap materials and charge exorbitant prices for them. There is dishonesty in the political field – for instance, a politician flying economy and reporting first class travel. There is dishonesty in the economic field, as charging more for goods than necessary. Lying and cursing are the order of the day. There is a desperate need to practice what one professes. In all of this, how wonderful and comforting to note Love's Final Solution.

REVELATION 10

Time No Longer

God's Word Important

There is a tendency that one might become dis-interested in the Revelation because of sameness, but every word is important in God's movement. It has eternal value and we must thank God for John, the beloved disciple, who wrote it down for our edification. There are times, in my study of Revelation, that my mind is so overwhelmed, that I scarcely know where I am. I am amazed at Love's Final Solution.

Here we have a parenthetical passage. It explains certain events not recorded in the seals nor trumpets nor the vials of wrath.

Delay No Longer

Between the sixth and seventh trumpet judg-ments there transpire certain things: The seventh trumpet does not sound until chapter 11:15. This angel, here, is not one of the seven nor of the four, but is like the other strong angel in chapter 5:2 and 18:21, or the other angel in chapter 14:6,15.

This angel is a special messenger of God's, and the burden of his message is "there shall be delay (time) no longer" (vs. 6). The size of the angel delivering the message is colossal, for he bestrides both land and sea. Man's time is running out. The Greek word for "time" is *chronos* meaning "clock time." The other Greek word for time is *chairos* meaning a life span or season or intensity of time flowing into a limited time period. Chronos time may be unlimited time as here designated. God can cause time to run out as far as the works of man are concerned.

Man Accountable

John sees what transpires on earth and he also is made to realize the important duties of the angels. The rainbow signifies what God asked for in Genesis 9. He holds the earth responsible and accountable for breaking the everlasting covenant, of which the rainbow was the token. The face of the angel shone as the sun (vs. 1). It shows the searching character of the angel. All is revealed in his sight and presence.

A Mystery

What the seven thunders uttered is being sealed. John would write or was about to write but was forbidden to write. The mystery of God shall not be revealed but shall be finished when the seventh angel shall sound. These shall yet be revealed in God's plan. A man can walk in a godly way and this is the "mystery of godliness," unknown to the world. The "mystery of lawlessness" is still being restrained (2 Thess. 2). Here, in this chapter, is the answer to the age old question, "Why did God allow man to sin?" Chapter 11:15 shows that righteousness finally will reign and His people will understand. The devil had his day.

The Seventh Trumpet Meaning

When the seventh angel sounds (vs. 7), all this mystery shall be finished. Here apparently the whole purpose of God in human history is meant – about the Fall of man, the regeneration, the restoration of both men and nature. So we expect the antichrist to appear and Israel to be hated and persecuted of all nations and Satan universally worshiped. And we shall expect God to manifest His anger. "Delay no longer" is the word.

The Open Book

The book of verse eight is open and not sealed. The word of the prophets has been open a long time and should have been studied. Because of the contents of wrath, judgment and hell and punishment, many have lost interest in the book of Revelation. The little book here is open, and one wonders if it could not be the book that Daniel was told to "seal up" (Dan. 12:4,9). It was for the "Time of the end," and not the "End of time." It was the "end" of the "Times of the Gentiles," the last half of the seventieth week. It was deliverance for Daniel's people and the setting up of the Kingdom. No great distinction is to be made here between *laleo* and *lego*, for "spake" and (vs. 8) "said." When eating the book, it was sweet to his taste (John's) but bitter to his stomach. "Every revelation of God's purposes, even though a mere fragment, is bitter-sweet, disclosing judgment as well as mercy" (Swete).

An Elect Nation

God's own, like John, saw what the remnant of Israel must suffer under the rage of Satan. This also shows us (vs. 11) that blessings to the nations of the earth are dependent upon how they treat Israel, the elect nation. Paul, in writing to the Roman church, said: "For I am not ashamed of the gospel of Christ: for it is the power of God unto salvation to every one that believeth; to the Jew first, and also to the Greek" (Rom. 1:16). Christ "will turn away the ungodliness from Jacob," and Israel will receive the favour to become national Israel as "life from the dead." Romans 11:26 says: "And so all Israel shall be saved: as it is written, there shall come out of Sion the Deliverer, and shall turn away ungodliness from Jacob." And Acts 15:16-17 notes: "After this I will return, and will build again the tabernacle of David, which is fallen down; and I will build again the ruins thereof, and I will set it up: that the residue of men might seek after the Lord, and all the Gentiles, upon whom my name is called, saith the Lord, who doeth all these things."

The Treaty

Apostate Israel will make a covenant and treaty with God's enemy, but God is already bringing about a change in chapter eleven. There is the measuring of the temple of God. The two witnesses will put the fear of God in the remnant of Israel. Just as God allowed them to be enemies concerning the Gospel, so the Gentiles could be saved; so now, God gives them election to be a blessing to the Gentile nations, so that God's mercy may have been extended to all alike and no one can be without excuse. This is Love's Final Solution.

The Times of the Gentiles

Joel, the prophet, refers to "multitudes, multitudes in the valley of decision," as he deals with the "Times of the Gentiles," during the tribulation. This has nothing to do with the expression "The fullness of the Gentiles" of Romans 11. The fullness of the Gentiles refers to those of the Gentiles who are saved and belong to the church body. The times of the Gentiles shall end in forty-two months here in Scripture; at Armageddon; at the plain of Megiddo (Aesdrellon valley).

Not Made With Hands

The language used in this chapter is Jewish. Stephen, for the Church, says: "The Most High dwelleth not in temples made with hands," and Paul and Peter say in 1 Corinthians 3, Ephesians 2 and 1 Peter 2:5 that the Church is, at *present*, the temple of God in which the Holy Spirit resides.

The Temple

Also, the Scripture reminds us that the only visible temple recognized by God is the one to be built in Jerusalem where the altar is for sacrifice and in which the antichrist will offer unclean offerings for a period of time.

The Temple and Gentiles

Other Scriptures in the Bible have prophesied a restoration and returning of the Jews to their land in unbelief but with a national consciousness. Zephaniah 2:1-2 says: "Gather yourselves together, yea, gather together, o nation not desired: before the decree bring forth, before the day pass as the chaff before the fierce anger of the Lord come upon you, before the day of the Lord's anger come upon you." This Scripture indicates what will be the spiritual condition of those who "gather themselves together" as a nation in the last days. With the recognition of Israel, the Gentiles take their place without (vs. 2), and they shall trample the city for three and a half years.

Before the Seventh Trumpet

There is here an interlude before the seventh trumpet. There are three points in the interlude: the chastisement of Jerusalem or Israel (vs. 1-2), the mission of the two witnesses (vs. 3-12), and the rescue of the remnant (vs. 13).

Temples

There are five temples named and foretold in history and prophecy:

1. *Solomon's temple.* 1 Kings 7:51 says: "So was ended all the work that king Solomon made for the house of the Lord. And Solomon brought in the things which David his father had dedicated;

even the silver, and the gold, and the vessels, did he put among the treasures of the house of the Lord."

2. *Zerubbable's temple.* Haggai 1:14 says: "And the Lord stirred up the spirit of Zerubbable the son of Shealtiel, the governor of Judah, and the spirit of Joshua the son of Josedech, the high priest, and the spirit of all the remnant of the people; and they came and did work in the house of the Lord of hosts, their God."

3. *Herod's temple.* John 2:19-20 says: "Jesus answered and said unto them, destroy this temple, and in three days I will raise it up. Then said the Jews, forty and six years was this temple in building, and wilt thou rear it up in three days?" (with reference to the temple that Herod built).

4. *The future Jewish temple in the days of the antichrist.* Daniel 9:27 says: "And he shall confirm the covenant with many for one week: and in the midst of the week he shall cause the sacrifice and the oblation to cease and for the overspreading of abominations he shall make it desolate, even until the consummation, and that determined shall be poured upon the desolate."

5. *The millennial temple.* Ezekiel 40:2a. says: "In the visions of God brought he me into the land of Israel." And in chapter 44:27 it says: "And in the day that he goeth into the sanctuary, unto the inner court, to minister in the sanctuary, he shall offer his sin offering, saith the Lord God."

The Outer Court

The outer court is left to its fate. In Herod's temple the outer court was marked off from the inner by "the middle wall of partition," beyond which a Gentile could not go. In this outer court was a house of prayer for the Gentiles, but now John is to cast it out and leave it to its fate to be profaned by them. "And the Holy city shall they tread under foot forty and two months" (vs. 2).

A Desolate House

Today it is still true what Jesus said: "Your house is left unto you desolate" (Matt. 23:38). Today there is no distinction between Jew or Gentile (Greek) but the church-age having ended (Rev. 4:1), God now proceeds to final things. And Israel is recognized, but chastening must come before repentance. The Gentiles will be dealt with by the Lord, as well, His people shall have national restoration. The duration of the beast desecrating the temple (3 1/2 years) will end with the testimony of the two witnesses. It is impossible to hurt these two witnesses till they do their work. The beast has its time, but that time shall end after 3 1/2 years when the beast shall break the covenant made with Israel in order that God's plan and purpose may be fulfilled in the vials of wrath to be outpoured.

The Two Witnesses

The two witnesses are the last witnesses before the earth is given over to the antichrist for a short period. Some claim that these two witnesses are

Enoch and Elijah. Others claim they are Moses and Elijah. Let us look at them more closely. They are two men, not covenants, nor the Church nor dispensations (vs. 3, 7-12). They are Christ's witnesses (vs. 3). They will be given power when they appear on earth (vs. 3). They will be prophets (vs. 3,10), and they prophesy the last forty-two months (vs. 2). They are clothed in sackcloth (vs. 3). The dress suited the message. They are symbolized by two olive trees and two candlesticks (vs. 4). They are two men later translated. They will be invincible for three and a half years (vs. 5-7). Fire comes out of their mouths (vs. 5). They have power to stop rain and have power to turn water into blood and are able to bring plagues (vs. 6). When their witness is finished, the beast (antichrist) will kill them (vs. 7). Therefore they cannot be the Church. They must be two men who have never died. They remain dead for three and a half days and will then be resurrected (vs. 8-11). This proves that they must never have died before.

Spiritual Sodom

They appear in the city of Jerusalem, spiritually called Sodom and Egypt (vs. 8), where the prophets and Jesus were killed and crucified. Also where sin was atoned for and where sin cried to heaven. Here we have pleasure-seeking and godlessness. The majority of the nation will turn to the antichrist. But the witnesses will cry against the claims of the beast, whose claims are that man is to be deified or glorified. In like manner, in our day, when the U.S.A. secretary of health sent out a letter to stop the use of fetuses from abortions for transplants, a woman in the laboratory, working with transplants of fetuses, complained that the secretary was yielding to special interest groups. It shows clearly into whose hand humanism is playing. Even in our day there is a real hatred (visible and invisible) of all that which is really of God. But our work has to be done as God wants it done before He takes us.

About the Roman Empire

The beast (vs. 7), could be the last head of the revived Roman Empire, with which the European Common Market has to do. Here is a rush to the banner of Satan. Jubilant jollification results over the cessation of the activity of the two prophets. When the witnesses have finished their testimony and are killed by the beast, there is fiendish glee of Jew and Gentile, who no longer will have to endure the prophecies and dread miracles of these two prophets. Such a sense of relief is perhaps not seldom felt today by bad men when a preacher of righteousness is removed.

An Ascension

Like Jesus, the witnesses come to life. They ascend to heaven in a cloud and their enemies see them and fear. This Scripture may have reference to Ezekiel 37:5, to the valley of dry bones that came to life. God is able to call back into life even dried up bones of human beings. Nothing is impossible to Him. The ascension of these witnesses is in full view of their enemies, not just in the presence of a few friends as with Christ. Four things follow: there is a great earthquake. One tenth part of Jerusalem falls. Seven thousand are slain. This can be compared with Elijah's time. And the rest gave glory to God because of fear and miracles performed. Love's Final Solution is still at work. Verse fourteen shows that the second woe is past (the sixth trumpet, Rev. 9:12) and the third woe is the seventh trumpet which is to come quickly.

The Age-long Struggle

These witnesses seem to witness the first half of Daniel's seventieth week, but Israel will not accept Jesus until the end of the week as the One "whom they have pierced" (Zech. 12:10). In verse eleven of that same passage are these words: "In that day shall there be a great mourning in Jerusalem," and in verse twelve it says: "And the land shall mourn, every family apart." This is the certain and glorious outcome of the age-long struggle against Satan, who wields the kingdom of the world which he offered to Christ on the mountain for one act of worship. But Jesus scorned partnership with Satan in the rule of the world, and chose war, war to the end. Now the climax has come with Christ as Conqueror of the kingdom of this world for his Father. And He and the Son shall reign forever.

A Crisis

This portion of Scripture, Revelation 11:15-19, marks a crisis in God's dealings. It gives God's outline of the events that follow. We must take note of such expressions like: "Thy wrath" (vs. 18); "nations angry" (vs. 18); "taken to thee Thy great power" (vs. 18). This is the time when He shall "destroy them who destroy the earth" (vs. 18). It includes the overthrow of the beast and its armies at the end of chapter nineteen, and the destruction of Gog and Magog (Prince of Russia) not only at Armageddon but also at the end of the millennium in Revelation 20. It covers even the time of the dead to be judged and spans the great white throne judgment. The seventh angel's trumpet brings us to the portals of the new creation, to chapter 21, from here on yet to come.

The Seventh Trumpet

The twenty-four elders celebrate the event both in realization and anticipation. At the sounding of the trumpet, God's whole attitude changes from hidden to open exercised authority. The elders anticipate the subjugation of the enemies, yet to be accomplished. Verse fifteen, in the Greek, has "kingdom" rather than "kingdoms." It means that at the sounding of the seventh trumpet, the whole dominion of the world has become God's. "Thou hast taken thy power" shows the permanence of God's rule.

A Resume

In chapter five the sealed book was given to Christ. In chapters six to nine there were visitations of divine displeasure. But God's Christ remained in heaven. The souls under the altar are asked to wait. Men, meanwhile, repented not. The angel of chapter ten announces that "in the days of the voice of the seventh angel, God will finish

His mystery and will reveal His authority." Now, in verse fifteen, He takes His power, the Kingdom is His and He reigns forever. Heaven celebrates the event. What we are looking forward to will have come.

The Lord God

The elders address Him as "Adonai," Lord God, the strong One. He is also known as "Elohim" and "El Shaddai," God Almighty. "Who art and Who wast." No longer "Who is to come." (It is not in the Greek.) He has come and taken up power and the Kingdom. He is reigning at last. Verse seventeen shows that He reigned all the time.

Divine Control

Divine control is not acceptable to the world. Therefore the psalmist asks the question: "Why do the nations rage?" (Ps. 2). There are so many who were angry against divine control: Cain, Saul, Absalom, Ahab and Jezebel, Nebuchadnezzar, Haman, Nero, Stalin, Lenin, Hitler, etc.

Attitude and Deeds

In verse eighteen we have the culmination of wrath against God. The dead are to be judged. John apparently means both good and bad coincident with the resurrection and judgment (Rev. 14:15b). To every unsaved creature the judgment is given in view of the light he had and according to his attitude and deeds. The rewards go to His servants, the prophets and saints. It would seem that while the tribulation is in process, the rewards are meted out in heaven. "And to them that fear thy name, small and great." It is like the righteous of Matthew 25:37-39, who did not have much light, but yet "feared the Lord." What an encouragement for all who are rather slow in learning God's will and purpose.

Shadows

There is a temple in heaven. The one on earth was a pattern of the things in heaven. Hebrews 8:5 says: "Who serve unto the example and shadow of heavenly things, as Moses was admonished of God when he was about to make the tabernacle: for, see, saith he, that thou make all things according to the pattern showed to thee in the mount." The ark's pattern, too, was given to Israel; not to the Church, for the Church does not have to do with earthly temple worship, as Israel does. Of the Church it is said, "Your body is the temple of God" (1 Cor. 3:16).

An Open Temple

God is dealing with Israel and the nations in the tribulation. Thus the temple in heaven is opened. Israel is to be established as God's elect nation, but under punishment first. And all nations will be represented against Jerusalem to the battle of Armageddon. Therefore, Revelation 11:19 pictures the situation as "lightnings and voices and thunderings and an earthquake and great hail."

The seventh trumpet includes all that happens down to chapter twenty, verse three. Christ is to set up His Kingdom at the end of the seven years.

A Prophetic Calendar

We need here to consider the prophetic calendar. We begin with the rapture of the Church (1 Thess. 4:4-18; 1 Cor. 15; Rev. 4:1). The Holy Spirit is the restrainer of evil, through His body the Church, and is removed from the earth before the antichrist appears (2 Thess. 2). Then comes the invasion of Israel by Russia and her confederacy (Ezek. 38-39). The antichrist grasps world power (Dan. 7:24; 8:25; 11). The antichrist makes a seven year pact with Israel (Dan. 9:27; Ezek. 38:8). A world church unites with the antichrist and plays a dominant role in the early stages of the dictator's drive to global rule (Rev. 17). The 144,000 will be evangelists with the gospel of the Kingdom. Divine judgments from heaven begin to be poured out upon the earth as the tribulation begins (Rev. 6). A series of dramatic events occur at the three and a half year period, mid-point of the seven year (great tribulation) period. Satan will be cast out on the earth. There occurs also the wrath of the Lamb and the character of the antichrist is revealed (Rev. 12:7-13; Rev. 17:16-18). Another series of horrific events lead up to the final act of the seven year tribulation period, called the "bowls of wrath" (vials) (Rev. 16), which finally leads to the battle of Armageddon. Then Christ's millennial reign begins upon earth (Rev. 20:4-6; Ezek. 48). Israel's borders are extended from the Euphrates to the Nile. The temple will be rebuilt and the sacrifices restored as a teaching memorial for unborn generations to show the truth of Christ's redemptive work (Zech. 6:15).

Then comes Satan's final rebellion, defeat and sentence in the Great White Throne Judgment (Rev. 20:11-15). The Kingdom is turned back to God by Christ (1 Cor. 15:24-28). The present heaven and earth are purged with fire and a new eternal heaven and earth are created (2 Pet. 3:10). The reason for a new heaven and earth is clear; no sinful personage has been admitted therein.

The Woman and the Dragon

The Wonder in Heaven

In this chapter we deal with a woman that represents Israel. It is a great wonder in heaven, as Jesus said in John 4:48: "Then said Jesus unto him, except ye see signs and wonders, ye will not believe." The time frame could be the middle of the seventieth week of Daniel. The woman cannot be the virgin Mary nor the church. Israel is always spoken of as the wife of God in the Old Testament. In Isaiah 47:7-9 Israel is called a widow. In Isaiah 50:1 Israel is called a divorced woman. An adulterous wife in Jeremiah 3:1-25. But God said He would take her back again. When? That would be when He carries the battle of Armageddon for her and sets up His Kingdom.

Israel and the Church

The place in prophecy is Israelitish. The two witnesses have been stationed at Jerusalem, where temple worship is again practiced. The words "sun, moon and stars" remind us of

Joseph's dream (Gen. 37:9). This is a forecast of Israel in the last days. The Church cannot be spoken of in this way, for she was chosen "before the foundation of the world," and her glory cannot be described in terms of this present creation. The Church's Lord is in heaven whereas this woman's connection is with the solar system, viewed from earth. She is clothed with the sun, the moon being under her feet and a twelve star crown on her head which indicates the subjection of earth to her governmental glory. This belongs to Israel and the restoring of the earthly kingdom to Israel. Israel is here described, in verse two, and also in the prophets, as travailing in birth. When was the Church ever in such a condition? Micah 5:2-3 says: "But thou, Bethlehem Ephratah, though thou be little among the thousands of Judah, yet out of thee shall he come forth unto me that is to be ruler in Israel; whose goings forth have been from of old, from everlasting. Therefore will he give them up, until the time that she which travaileth hath brought forth: then the remnant of his brethren shall return unto the children of Israel."

Who are Israelites?

Israel, not the Church, gave birth to Christ. Paul, in writing to the Roman church, says in Romans 9:4-5: "Who are Israelites; to whom pertaineth the adoption, and the glory, and the covenants, and the giving of the law, and the service of God, and the promises; Whose are the fathers, and of whom as concerning the flesh Christ came, who is over all, God blessed forever."

The Roman church would like to accept this woman as the Church and many Christians would follow in this acceptance. That is why the woman and the child play a large roll in the Roman church. It is, however, a pagan concept. This would reverse the order of birth – the woman coming from the child, rather than the child coming from the woman. Some also feel that the Man-child is the 144,000. But these have never been exalted to the throne of God.

The Sign in Heaven Proceeds on Earth

This woman's history is on earth, persecuted by the enemy (vs. 13-16). It is the *sign* that is seen in heaven, while her experience proceeds on earth. It is to prepare her (Israel-woman) for her heavenly role (spiritual role) in the kingdom age, that she is persecuted on earth. Israel will flee to a place of safety, while her remnant (144,000) will be persecuted. The same expression is used in Revelation 12:17 as in Revelation 14:12.

Satan and the Child

This is "Jacob's trouble" of Israel in the last days (vs. 6), and coincides with Daniel's seventieth week. It is the great tribulation of three and a half years. Verses three and four show great wisdom (the number seven), and almost perfect power (governmental) (ten horns) of the Roman Empire. Satan drew a third part of stars and cast them on earth (perhaps they are the angels that followed Satan in the Fall) and now waits for the birth of the Child and tries to disrupt the whole purpose of God. Daniel 8:10 says: "And it waxed great, even to the host of heaven; and it cast down some of the host and of the stars to the ground, and stamped upon them." And verse 24 says: "And his power shall be mighty, but not by his own power: and he shall destroy wonderfully, and shall prosper, and practice and shall destroy the mighty and the holy people." This is his aim and his occupation.

Christ the Man-Child

The child can be no one but Christ, who was to rule all nations. Psalm 2 says: "Why do the heathen rage... the kings of the earth set themselves... against the Lord, and against his anointed... the Lord hath said unto me, Thou art my son; this day have I begotten thee.... Ask of me, and I shall give thee the heathen for thine inheritance... thou shalt break them with a rod of iron." Revelation 19:15 says: "And out of his mouth goeth a sharp sword, that with it he should smite the nations: and he shall rule them with a rod of iron: and he treadeth the winepress of the fierceness and wrath of Almighty God." What Satan tried to do with Christ is history to us, but is related here to show the whole plan of God. Satan, for that reason, tried to destroy the male line of man (Moses and later the male children under two years of age at Bethlehem). The child is taken up to God and His throne. Stephen saw Christ standing at the throne of God as he was stoned to death.

Between verses five and six may stand the church-age. This is the gap between the sixty-ninth and seventieth weeks of Daniel.

The Dragon

Ezekiel 28:11-19 describes the dragon in by-gone days: 'Thou wast perfect in the ways from the day that thou wast created, till iniquity was found in thee... thine heart was lifted up because of thy beauty... thou shalt be a terror, and never shalt thou be any more." There never was such a king Tyrus with such a fall. Even Michael, the archangel durst not bring against him railing accusation. Satan seems to have been of a higher order of being than angels. Jude 9 says of Satan, "Yet Michael the archangel, when contending with the devil, disputed about the body of Moses, durst not bring against him a railing accusation, but said, The Lord rebuke thee." Isaiah 14:12-13 says: "How art thou fallen from heaven, O Lucifer, son of the morning... for thou hast said in thine heart, I will ascend into heaven, I will exalt my throne above the stars of God... I will be like the most High... yet thou shalt be brought down to hell – to the sides of the pit."

Red Satan

Satan is seen as "red" (vs. 3). It is the colour of murder and blood. The Lord says of him "he was a murderer from the beginning." He has an awful history. Pride caused his apostasy. Hatred, deceit and violence continue in his wake, even after the millennium. Revelation 20:7-8: "And when the thousand years are expired, Satan shall be loosed out of his prison, and shall go out to deceive the nations which are in the four quarters of the earth, Gog and Magog, to gather them together to battle: the number of whom is as the sand of the sea." The only ones that will escape Satan's terror as nations, are Edom and Moab in the Jordan area. Perhaps "Petra" will be a place of refuge for Israel. Isaiah 16:1 has the term "Sela" for "Petra" and Amos 1:12 has the term "Bozrah" for "Petra." Petra speaks of the rock or place in Edom. Verse seventeen of chapter twelve shows that this is not spoken of the Church for she leaves *no remnant behind.*

Iniquity Found

He (Satan) is called a Dragon in verse four and reveals the hideousness and horror of sin. This aspect of Satan can be compared with the beauty he had before his fall. Ezekiel 28:15 says: "Thou wast perfect in thy ways from the day that thou wast created, till iniquity was found in thee." Dragon is used only in Revelation where it appears thirteen times – twelve times concerning Satan.

Ten Horns and Satan

In chapter 13:1, we see the likeness and the distinction between Satan and his final world power, developed by Satan and headed by the fearful man of Revelation 13:18. While the seven heads are there, it is the ten horns that rule with the antichrist. Satan has projected his plan of universal earth-rule by ten kings. It is the final form of the fourth world-power of Daniel 7. The seven heads and seven crowns (diadems) of chapter 12:3, show complete wisdom of revenge and wrath of Satan which he gives to ten kings to revenge him on Israel. Daniel 9:24 says: "Seventy weeks are determined upon thy people and upon thy holy city, to finish the transgression, and to make an end of sins, and to make reconciliation for iniquity, and to bring in everlasting righteousness, and to seal up the vision and prophecy, and to anoint the most Holy." And verse fourteen of chapter ten says: "Now I am come to make thee understand what shall befall thy people in the latter days: for yet the vision is for many days."

A Defiled Being

When we consider the hundred million angels and millions upon millions after that, of Revelation 5:11, who remained true to God, we get some idea of the host, who by Satan were drawn away. Ezekiel 28:16-19 reads: "By the multitude of thy merchandise they have filled the midst of thee with violence, and thou hast sinned: therefore I will cast thee as profane out of the mountain of God: and I will destroy thee, O covering cherub, from the midst of the stones of fire. Thine heart was lifted up because of thy beauty, thou hast corrupted thy wisdom by reason of thy brightness: I will cast thee to the ground, I will lay thee before kings, that they may behold thee. Thou hast defiled thy sanctuaries by the multitude of thine iniquities, by the iniquity of thy traffick; therefore will I bring forth a fire from the midst of thee, it shall devour thee, and I will bring thee to ashes upon the earth in the sight of all them that behold thee. All they that know thee among the people shall be astonished at thee: thou shalt be a terror, and never shalt thou be any more."

The Aim of Satan

The dragon wants to devour the Child (vs. 4). This is in retrospect, looking back to the time when Christ was born and Satan, through Herod the king, wanted to slay the babe. Satan, realizing Christ's destiny to rule all nations with a rod of iron, wanted to devour or destroy Him. Zechariah 9:9-10 reads as follows: "Rejoice greatly, O daughter of Zion; shout, O daughter of Jerusalem: behold, thy King cometh unto thee: he is just and having salvation; lowly, and riding upon an ass, and upon a colt the foal of an ass. And I will cut off the chariot from Ephraim, and the horse from Jerusalem, and the battle bow shall be cut off: and he shall speak peace unto the heathen: and his dominion shall be from sea even to sea, and from the river even to the ends of the earth."

Three Scenes

There are three scenes in Revelation 12.

1. Christ is born to Israel and ascended, despite the dragon, to await His rule over the nations (vs. 1-5).

2. The casting out of Satan and his angels from all places in heaven and the resulting joy of heaven (vs. 7-12).

3. The persecution of the woman (Israel) and her seed and then her protection for 1260 days (the great tribulation) which may be at Petra.

War in Heaven

Verse seven shows war in heaven by Michael and his angels against the dragon and his angels.

Michael (Jude 9) is the archangel assigned by God to care for Israel. Daniel 12:1 says: "And at that time shall Michael stand up, the great prince which standeth for the children of *thy* people; and there shall be a time of trouble, such as never was since there was a nation even to that same time: and at that time *thy* people shall be delivered, every one that shall be found written in the book."

The Accuser of the Brethren

The accuser of the brethren is cast on the earth: verse nine gives his various names. He is that old serpent from the garden of Eden. He is the devil who tempted Jesus in Matthew 4. He is Satan that deceives the whole world and he is the accuser. It is good to know that Christ is the "Advocate" before the Father for us. He, Jesus, speaks good for us and Satan knows that we shall judge angels. 1 Corinthians 6:3a says, "Know ye not that we shall judge angels?"

Churches Are Not the Kingdom

Although the verb in verse eleven is in the past tense, "overcame," the verse deals with those who on earth are overcomers – "Who loved not their lives unto the death." People who speak of certain of their churches as "kingdom hall" are rather ahead of themselves. Christ has not as yet set up His Kingdom (vs. 10). Satan is still the prince of this age.

Satan and Israel

Verses 13-17 show Jacob's trouble. Satan knows that his time for doing harm is limited, and hence his great wrath (thumon-boiling rage). Satan hates Israel. They are God's elect people and because of that nation is Christ. Paul says in Romans 9:4-5, "Who are Israelites; to whom pertaineth the adoption, and the glory, and the covenants, and the giving of the law, and the service of God, and the promises; Whose are the fathers, and of whom as concerning the flesh Christ came, who is over all, God blessed for ever." Christ is to have the Kingdom upon Satan's overthrow. Here is Love's Final Solution.

God's Protection

Satan sends armies after Israel. Miraculous cataclysms aid Israel. Sandstorms can overcome armies and helicopters. God is able to protect His own. Then Satan makes war on any other godly people left in Jerusalem and the 144,000 who keep the commandments and have accepted Christ, the Messiah (Rev. 12:17 and 14:12). Two similar expressions are found here.

The Beast and His Prophet

The Beast

The Lord Jesus said: "I came not to judge the world, but to save the world." We come now to consider those who would damn the world. In Revelation 11:7 we have the beast out of the abyss. Here we have the wild beast from the sea, as in Daniel 7:23, a vast empire is used in the interest of brute force. This beast, like the dragon (12:3) has ten horns and seven heads, but the horns are crowned, not the heads. The Roman Empire seems to be meant where the Roman emperors had "theos" (god) constantly applied to them.

The Fourth Empire

Here, in verses one and two we see the revival of the fourth Empire in its last form. Daniel saw in a vision the four world empires, as Babylon, Media-Persia, Greece and Rome (Dan. 7). In the last verse of Revelation 13, we have the number 666 – the number of the beast and it is the number of a man. The beast is the production of the devil, upon his fury of being cast out from heaven to earth. Let us consider the beast (antichrist). The beast combines features of the first three beasts in Daniel 7:2. The strength and brutality of the Babylonian, Median and Persian Empires appeared in the Roman Empire. The catlike vigilance of the leopard, the slow and crushing power of the bear, and the roar of the lion. The dragon (Satan) works through the beast. The beast will be a man (vs. 18). He will rise out of the sea of humanity (nations) (vs. 1) and Daniel 7:24. He will become ruler of the area of the seven kingdoms symbolized by the seven heads (vs. 1-17). He will become ruler of the ten kingdoms of the Old Roman Empire (Common Market) (vs. 1). He will be a blasphemer (vs. 1,5). The little horn of Daniel 7:8 will be a leader and will overcome three of the first *ten* kingdoms and he will be the eighth. He will receive his power, throne and great authority from Satan (2:13-16). His one head is wounded to death and is healed. All the world will wonder at him (vs. 2-4). He will be an object of worship. He imitates Christ's death and resurrection. He will be a great orator (vs. 5-6). He will be given power for 42 months (vs. 5). He will defy God and claim to be God (vs. 6). He will make war on Jews and Christians (saved in the tribulation). Multitudes will be killed (vs. 7). He will be given power over all nations inside the ten kingdoms of the Old Roman Empire (revived) territory (vs. 7-8). The beast (antichrist) will have a religious leader in the False Prophet of verses 11-17 and 16:13-16. He will permit image worship (Emperor worship) which is devil-worship. It can be classified as self-worship (humanism). He will cause the mark of his kingdom, or his name, or the number of his name to be branded upon the right hand or forehead of his followers (vs. 16-18). The name of the beast is not stated. Since it is the name of a man, some have guessed at he being Judas, the Pope, Mussolini, Hitler, Napoleon, Stalin and others. The number of this man is 666.

The Work of the Restrainer Changed – The Beast Rules

The restrainer of 2 Thessalonians 2:7 has been removed in the rapture. In Revelation 4:5, John sees the seven spirits (fullness of the Holy Spirit) in heaven. But He will come and leave as in the Old Testament during the tribulation, so that people can be redeemed. From Daniel 2:42,44 and 7:24 we know that the ten toes were to be ten kings. The ten horns of Revelation 13:1 correspond to those of Daniel and Revelation 17:3 and are interpreted in Revelation 17:12. The ten horns are ten kings and receive authority (power, throne) with the beast (antichrist) for one hour. On these horns (ten kings) are the diadems (a band around the head) which show distinct powers. The beast can kill the two witnesses, 11:7-12. He (Satan through the beast) can change times and laws. Daniel 7:25 says: "And he shall speak great words against the most High, and shall wear out the saints of the most High, and think to change times and laws: and they shall be given into his hand until a time and times and the dividing of time." He understands mysteries. Daniel 8:23 says: "And in the latter time of their kingdom, when the transgressors are come to the full, a king of fierce countenance, and understanding dark sentences, shall stand up." He does as he wills for a period of time. Daniel 11:36 says: "And the king shall do according to his will; and he shall exalt himself, and magnify himself above every god, and shall speak marvellous things against the God of gods, and shall prosper till the indignation be accomplished: for that that is determined shall be done." He performs miracles (Rev. 13:1-8). He causes craft to prosper and controls money and commerce. Daniel 8:25a says: "And through his policy also he shall cause craft to prosper in his hand." He reigns for forty-two months (13:5). The people worship Satan who gives power to the beast (antichrist). To secure the worship of men, Satan is aided by the antichrist and the false prophet.

Satan Imitates God's Plan

The Greek word for "slain" (vs. 3) in the King James Bible, "wounded," is the same in chapter 5:6 "a lamb... as though it had been slain" and as in chapter 13:3 "wounded." Satan imitates God's plan. Here, part of a killed body has arisen and that part of body has been entered by the beast and he is the eighth ruler of Revelation 17:11. "And the beast that was, and is not, even he is the eighth, and is of the seven, and goeth into perdition."

Seven Heads

The seven heads, according to Revelation 17, are seven mountains upon which the woman sits and it goes on to say they are seven kings – five are fallen, one is, the other is not yet come. This head, here in Revelation 13, that was wounded, is one of the seven Roman emperors of which five had fallen when John wrote. One Domitian was reigning, the seventh had not yet come in John's time. He comes out of the abyss where the departed spirits are and the world is surprised and they worship Satan who gives life to the beast (antichrist). One wonders, what will all come out of the Roman Empire? Verses five and six reveal that which all men look for: wisdom, intelligence and, of all things, blasphemies against Christ and His Church in heaven. Those who oppose the beast on earth will die, or be captured.

Names of Beast in Old Testament

The beast is called by various names in the Old Testament.

1. *The Assyrian.* Isaiah 10:5 says: "O Assyrian, the rod of mine anger."

2. *The King of Babylon.* Isaiah 14:4 says: "That thou (Israel) shalt take up this proverb against the king of Babylon, and say, How hath the oppressor ceased!"

3. *Lucifer.* Isaiah 14:12 says: "How art thou fallen from heaven, O Lucifer, son of the morning."

4. *The little horn.* Daniel 7:8a says: "There came up among them another little horn... and, behold, in this horn were eyes like the eyes of man, and a mouth speaking great things."

5. *A king of fierce countenance.* Daniel 8:23 says: "And in the latter time of their kingdom, when the transgressors are come to the full, a king of

fierce countenance, and understanding dark sentences, shall stand up."

6. *The prince that shall come.* Daniel 9:26 says: "And after threescore and two weeks shall Messiah be cut off, but not for himself: and the people of the prince that shall come shall destroy the city and the sanctuary."

7. *The willful king.* Daniel 11:36 says: "And the king shall do according to his will; and he shall exalt himself, and magnify himself above every god, and shall speak marvellous things against the God of gods."

In the New Testament

In the New Testament the beast is called:

1. *The man of sin.* 2 Thessalonians 2:3 says: "Let no man deceive you by any means: for that day shall not come, except there come a falling away first, and that man of sin be revealed, the son of perdition."

2. *The son of perdition,* so called in the above description.

3. *That Wicked.* 2 Thessalonians 2:8: "And then shall that Wicked be revealed whom the Lord shall consume with the spirit of his mouth, and shall destroy with the brightness of his coming."

4. *The antichrist.* 1 John 2:18 says: "Little children, it is the last time: and as ye have heard that antichrist shall come, even now are there many antichrists; whereby we know that it is the last time."

5. *The beast* (Rev. 13:1-2).

The Second Beast

The second beast out of the earth (vs. 11), is also of the satanic trinity. Both beasts are humans. They are cast into the lake of fire later on. The "sea" may have reference to the Mediterranean, around whose shores the four great earth empires had their existence. But in Revelation 13 the sea means universal recognition. The leader of the revived Roman Empire will play a part in this arena.

The False Prophet

The beast (antichrist) is operating at Jerusalem for the first half of Daniel's seventieth week (Rev. 11:9). The second beast is his prophet. Let us consider him as well. He, also, will be a man. In chapter 13:11, the word "*allos*" in the Greek means "another of the same kind." It can apply to the second beast. He will come out of the earth (vs. 11), the underworld. He will be a prophet of the first beast (vs. 12; 16:13). He will come with a lamb-like appearance without the ferocity of the other beast, but will speak like a dragon. With the power of the first beast, he will cause all to worship the first beast (vs. 12). He will perform miracles and deceive men (vs. 13-14). He will cause men to make an image of the first beast to be worshiped (vs. 14). He gives life to the image, to speak (vs. 15). Christ warned His disciples against false prophets and false christs with their signs and wonders. Mark 13:22 says: "For false christs and false prophets shall arise, and shall show signs and wonders to seduce, if it were possible, even the elect." He (the last beast) will cause the image to demand the death penalty for all who will not worship the antichrist (vs. 15). He will cause men to accept a mark (vs. 16). No one can buy or sell if no brand is accepted (vs. 17). He will be equal to the first beast in sending demon spirits, to gather the nations to Armageddon (16:13-16). He will still be conscious, as the first beast, in the lake of fire, one thousand years later (20:10).

A Syrian

In Isaiah 10:12 and 14:25, the antichrist is shown as a Syrian. Could he be a Syrian Jew with Roman citizenship, since Israel will accept the three and a half year covenant that the antichrist offers? In all of this, some will not accept the worship of the image of the beast and will be killed. This is Love's Final Solution. Always some will accept God's way and die for Him (vs. 15). The number of the beast is the number and name of a man, but what man and what a name. The world waits for him.

REVELATION 14

The Lamb and the 144,000

This chapter is parenthetical (something put in beside, explanatory, intervening occurrence). It shows the Lamb on Mount Sion with the 144,000 who have the name of the Lamb and God upon their foreheads, rather than the mark of the beast. These would seem to be the same as those of chapter seven. John sees them as part of the remnant of Israel, who present the gospel of the Kingdom during the tribulation, both men and women.

Firstfruits

They are the "firstfruits" of the millennium. They have passed through the fearful divine judgments and through the horrors of the first forty-two months of the antichrist (chapter 13). They are seen by John on Mount Sion (vs. 1). This is a selected seat of the glorious earthly reign of one thousand years of Christ and His saints and these 144,000.

Seen on Mount Sion, they will shortly, after the last three and a half years, share Christ's reign. They are the first of the harvest of the tribulation period that will come into the millennium.

A Complete Number

Seven things are told us about this company:

1. The name of the Lamb and God is written on their foreheads (vs. 1), so that all may see. It proclaimed their ownership.

2. They learned the new song (vs. 3). It was begun in Revelation 5:9-10. Only one exultation is greater (Rev. 19) – that of the Bride. The song is so profound because of the sufferings gone through.

3. They had been purchased out of the earth (vs. 3). They will reign on earth with the Lamb and His Church, being heavenly minded.

4. They are virgins (vs. 4). They kept themselves also clean from the sin of fornication. The Greek word "*parthenos*" can be applied to both men and women. Marriage, here, is excluded. The New Testament exalts marriage and this passage does not degrade it. There is also a Mount Sion in heaven. Hebrews 12:22 says: "But ye are come unto Mount Sion, and unto the city of the living God, the heavenly Jerusalem, and to an innumerable company of angels." But the millennium is on earth.

5. They follow the Lamb. There is oneness of mind.

6. They are firstfruits (vs. 4). They are not the Church nor Gentile believers, as some groups maintain. They are Israelites. These words here are Kingdom words and have nothing to do with salvation words.

7. They are without blemish (fault) (vs. 5). They
are not of the falsehood of the antichrist. In
their mouth was no lie. Zephaniah 3:13 says:
"The remnant of Israel shall not do iniquity,
nor speak lies; neither shall a deceitful tongue
be found in their mouth; for they shall feed and
lie down, and none shall make them afraid."
This deals with the restoration of Israel in
process here.

The Everlasting Gospel

During the days of antichrist (chapters 13-18)
the "everlasting gospel" is preached by the angel,
calling men to judgment (vs. 7). It reminds us that
the law was given by angels. Galatians 3:19 says:
"Wherefore then serveth the law? It was added
because of transgression till the seed should come
to whom the promise was made; and it was
ordained by angels in the hand of a mediator."

Forsaking God for Other Gods

Verses six and seven are good news to Israel
and all those dwelling on earth who have passed
through judgment, that their troubles will soon be
over. In verse eight Babylon's doom is announced.
Idolatry is the sin here and in John's time it was
emperor worship. Fornication, here in Revelation
14, means leaving God and following other gods. It
was a test of loyalty to Christ. The people of God
are to come out of her.

Doom

In verses nine to twelve we see the doom of
antichrist's followers. The white heat of God's

anger, held back through the ages, will be turned loose. It is strong wine mixed with spices to make it still stronger. Here we see God withdrawing all mercy forever. The enemies shall drink of the wrath of God. They shall be tormented with fire. They have not observed Love's Final Solution. The onlookers are the angels and the Lamb. The duration is forever (as ordained by God according to His determination). Their day of grace is past. The saints are the remnant of Israel. They must wait and suffer, it seems. Those who have the mark of the beast, have no rest for three and a half years. But for the martyrs there is rest. The test of loyalty to Christ is being rewarded. They rest from the toils, the weariness, but not from the activities. Heaven is not a place of idleness, but of the highest form of spiritual service.

Death Better Than Life

These are days of antichrist tyranny. Therefore death is better than life (vs. 13). John is asked to "write." No doubt, he was sick at heart over the sight of what has befallen his people. Rest, in those days, is obtained in no other way but death. Daniel 7:25 comes here in focus, "And he (antichrist) shall speak great words against the most High, and shall wear out the saints of the most High, and think to change times and laws; and they shall be given into his hand until a time and times and the dividing of time (3 1/2 years)." Then, also, their works accompany them. These martyrs get a higher place than Israel who merely inherit the Kingdom (Matt. 25:31-46). Again, to write means "emphasis" of what is foretold and occurring.

Harvesting

Then in verses 14-20 we have the harvest, a vision of Armageddon. To sit on the "white cloud" shows Christ's position (vs. 14). Jesus was the Sower and is also the Reaper. It is the harvesting of the earth. "Thrust in thy sickle" the angel urges. This is the harvest of the Gentile nations, being prepared for Revelation 16:13-16. The golden crown shows Him as the God-appointed King. He has a reaping instrument – the sickle. In verse seventeen we see the fifth angel with a sharp sickle to gather the vintage as Christ did the wheat. It is the angel of vengeance and he responds to the call of the sixth angel here as Christ does to the call of the fourth angel.

In Matthew 13:47-52 we have the wicked gathered by angels for punishment while the righteous remain on earth, where the Kingdom is set up. Luke 23:30-31 says: "Then shall they begin to say to the mountains, fall on us: and to the hills, cover us. For if they do these things in a green tree, what shall be done in the dry?" This shows clearly what will happen to Israel in the last days. If they do these things in a green tree (crucifying Christ), what shall be done in the dry?" (His followers).

The Place of Reckoning

Verses 18-19 show us the same vision as Joel 3:12-14 gives us.

"Let the heathen be wakened, and come up to the valley of Jehoshaphat: for there will I sit to judge all the heathen round about. Put in the sickle, for the harvest is ripe: come, get you down: for the press is full, the vats overflow; for their wickedness is great. Multitudes, multitudes, in the valley of decision: for the day of the Lord is near in the valley of decision." They are in the valley of decision (Megiddo, Jezreel, Esdraelon, the plain between Galilee on the north and Samaria on the south. It connects with the Jordan valley). Here in Revelation, they gather at Armageddon, and here the antichrist and his forces will be judged (defeated).

Esdraelon was the scene of some of the most important battles in Bible history: the victory of Barak over Sisera (Judges 4) and of the Philistines over Saul and his sons (1 Sam. 31). Here, also, the Egyptians mortally wounded Josiah, king of Judah (2 Kings 23:29). A great future is indicated for this area.

Blood

Outside Jerusalem (the city) blood shall flow for 200 miles. This blood-bath may come from man and water turned to blood or even rain of blood. Ezekiel speaks of the Lord fighting against Gog and says: "And I will plead against him with pestilence and with blood: and I will rain upon him, and upon his bands, and upon the many people that are with him, an overflowing rain, and great hailstones, fire and brimstone" (38:22). But the blood is a reminder of Love's Final Solution.

REVELATION 15

The Seven Last Plagues

In chapters fifteen and sixteen we consider certain particulars preceding the Great Day of Wrath and Armageddon. In Revelation 14:8, Babylon is announced as fallen, but only in anticipation. Now in Revelation 16:19 in the seventh vial she is being judged as she is remembered by God.

The Last Seven Plagues

In chapter fifteen "another sign" shows the seven last wrath angels and the rejoicing because of the victory over the beast (vs. 2-4). It is a moving experience to listen to a great orchestra. The great moment comes when the conductor calls in all instruments until the symphony is brought to its climax with every musician playing his part. There must be quality in our personal worship. In Revelation 15 we have the personal victory of certain of God's servants over the beast and they sing the song of Moses and of the Lamb, and as they sing, heaven opens, for this is the result of true quality in worship and of personal sacrifice. They realize Love's Final Solution in the acts of God.

Seven last plagues means finality and complete-ness.

The Old and New

John combines here the song of Moses and the song of the Lamb. He combines the expressions of the old and the new in the song to the glorified Messiah (vs. 3), because God alone is perfectly holy (vs. 4).

Personal Worship

Look at God's order in personal worship. The sons of the morning shouted for joy in creation. The angels sang at the birth of the Redeemer. All this to add to the throng that shall praise God in eternity. The early Christians died for their faith. That was the quality of their personal worship. It must be sincere and active. Job said: "The Lord gave, the Lord hath taken away, blessed be the name of the Lord." But we see here also the seven vials of wrath and the holy temple. All the world, it seems, is leaning toward devil worship and there-fore, there come from the open heaven, those who shall bring the judgments in the vials of wrath.

Trials Experienced

The sea, mingled with fire (vs. 2), reveals through what trials these saints had passed. The persecutions under the beast must have been ter-rible. The song of Moses celebrated the overthrow of Pharaoh and his army. In Moses' time the tem-ple was filled with the glory of the Lord and a cloud was over it (Exod. 40:34-36). But there was no smoke. The cloud meant "grace." The smoke here meant judgment (vs. 8). So does the presence of the temple. But in the new Jerusalem or new heaven and new earth there will be no temple. The tabernacle of testimony (vs. 5), shows that God is about to fulfill His covenant promises toward Israel. Romans 9:4 says: "Who are Israelites; to whom pertaineth the adoption, and the glory, and the covenants, and the giving of the law, and the service of God, and the promises."

Vindication

And now we come to the last plagues. The seven golden vials show the very glory of God. It is God's vindication of the holiness of the tribulation saints and He begins to punish those who follow the beast.

The Vial Judgments

God's Command

Similarity is here to be noted. Since no one could enter the temple (Greek: *naos*, shrine) but God, it is not an angel but God who orders the angels to pour out the vials of the wrath of God upon the earth. The *seven* angels show us a complete number and they show us also the tribulation being brought to a completion. Verse two shows the first angel pouring out the first vial. There came a bad and malignant sore upon those with the mark of the beast upon them and upon those who worshiped his image. A comparison of verse two may be made with the plague of Exodus 9:9 where in Egypt boils broke forth upon men. Here is God's Final Solution of Love. He saves the lost in sin and He also punishes those who reject His salvation and continue in sin without repentance. And the vial judgments come fast one upon another. We say again, they are God's vindication of the holiness of His people as He begins to punish those who follow the beast.

The Vial Judgments

Verse three shows the plague as being poured into the sea and, as in Egypt, all living things in the sea died. The first plague, though, in Egypt only affected the Nile; here all the earth was touched. The third angel (vs. 4) poured his vial upon the rivers and fountains and they became blood. In this we must recognize what we are doing today by way of pollution. It will be much worse, however, in the last days. They have shed blood and so they are worthy of their punishment. As the victim suffers and is slain, so the guilty receive just punishment. Psychologists and Psychiatrists and Lawyers and others of the legal profession, will not be handing down judgment, but One who is omniscient and makes no mistake. His judgments are true and righteous (vs. 7).

The Fourth and Fifth Vial

Science claims the sun is "cooling off." It does not seem to be doing so in verses eight and nine. The fourth trumpet affected a third of the sun, moon and stars with a plague of darkness (8:12), but here it is a plague of extreme heat. The word "fire" intensifies the act. Even deserved punishment may harden the heart. If grace cannot lead men to God, they will not be won. It would seem that human nature does not mend under judgment. They gnawed their tongues for pain and repented not. Rather they blaspheme God. The hardened human heart asserts itself and is something that is difficult to change. It can be a stubborn, defiant and obstinate organ, hardened by a continuous and willful determination to walk its own way. Rome was like that; power-hungry and merciless in its dealings. The fifth angel dealt with such action.

The Sixth Vial

The sixth angel poured his vial of wrath upon the river Euphrates and the waters of the river were dried up (vs. 12). The river was the eastern boundary of Israel as the Mediteranean sea is the western boundary. This river is nearly 1,780 miles long; from the Armenian mountains to the Persian Gulf. It flows through old Babylon, which may be rebuilt in the antichrist time period. It was seen just outside of Eden, we are told. Here sin began (Gen. 2:14) and is last seen in Revelation 16:12 where sin reaches its climax. It dries up so that the eastern armies can come into battle, along with other (Arab nations) to Armageddon. The armies of China, Japan, India etc. will come that way. The others are the Old Roman revived Empire under antichrist (Common Market); the king of the north (Ezek. 38 and 39) called Russia; the king of the south (Dan. 11:40). All of them against Christ and His angels. Verses 13-16 show the evil spirits as persuading the kings and nations to do battle. And these seducing evil spirits are sent out by the satanic trinity. These are deceiving spirits and teachings of demons. Let us not forget that the Egyptian magicians also wrought signs. In our day we must recognize the thousands of witches that ply their trade and devil worshippers and satanic churches. Their teachings have a tendency to creep into pulpits and Christian churches. But here, in this chapter, these spirits spur on the kings of the whole world to a real world war. But it is more likely a war against God.

As a Thief

Compare verse fifteen, "as a thief" with 1 Thessalonians 4:2 where the day of the Lord comes as a thief. But we, as the Church, are not looking for that day. We are looking for the Day of Christ. 2 Thessalonians 2:7-8 says: "For the mystery of iniquity doth already work: only 'He' who now letteth (hinders) will let (hinder), until he be taken out of the way. And then shall that Wicked be revealed, whom the Lord shall consume with the spirit of his mouth, and shall destroy with the brightness of his coming."

Armageddon is actually "Har-Magedon" (vs. 16). It means mountain of Megiddo. Here Barak overthrew the Canaanites (Judg. 5:19). This area is near Mount Carmel where Elijah killed the prophets of Baal. Also Mount Tabor is near. It is a vast plain that leads to the valley of Hinnom and Kidron.

The Seventh Vial

In verses 17-21 is shown the seventh vial which is poured out into the air and there is heard a great voice, saying: "It is done." This is followed by a great earthquake and the city of Jerusalem was divided into three parts and the cities of the nations fell. It all shows the destruction moving toward the end. The whole series of plagues is now complete. The three spirits from antichrist and the false prophet have brought

confusion and apostacy. Zechariah 14:4-5 foretold this earthquake here in chapter 16:18 when
he says: "And his feet shall stand in that day
upon the mount of Olives, which is before
Jerusalem on the east, and the mount of Olives
shall cleave in the midst thereof toward the east
and toward the west, and there shall be a very
great valley; and half of the mountain shall
remove toward the north, and half of it toward the
south. And ye shall flee toward the valley of the
mountains; for the valley of the mountains shall
reach unto Azal: yea, ye shall flee, like as ye fled
from before the earthquake in the days of Uzziah
king of Judah: and the Lord my God shall come,
and all the saints with thee." And at the same
time God remembers Babylon. God does not forget. As the seventh vial finishes the wrath of God,
we are told what will happen to the enemies of
God in chapters seventeen and eighteen. But here
in verse twenty-one, men blaspheme God and
repent not. Not even when they experience the
great hail, the weight of a talent (Greek: *talanton*)
from 708 to 730 pounds.

REVELATION 17

Judgment of Babylon

It is fitting that one of the seven angels that had the seven bowls should explain the judgment on Babylon. The word "*krima*" (judgment) is the one used about the doom of Babylon in Jeremiah 51:9 which says: "We would have healed Babylon, but she is not healed: forsake her, and let us go everyone into his own country: for her "judgment" reacheth unto heaven, and is lifted up even to the skies."

Corrupt Idolatry

It would seem that chapter seventeen deals with (mystical) Babylon. The term ecclesiastical is derived from "*ecclesia*," the Church. It was the seat of the most corrupt idolatry and the enemy of Christianity. It was some fifty miles south of modern Baghdad, in Iraq, on the Euphrates River. Here was a doctrine to quiet and set at ease the conscience. It is like apostate christendom or nominal Christianity. It is different from political Babylon of chapter eighteen, since in that chapter we have the beast's confederated empire. The last form of Gentile world-dominion. This system will destroy the former so that the beast may be the object of worship (2 Thess. 2:3-4). But the political Babylon is destroyed by the return of the Lord in glory.

Lovers

In verse two we see her sins and lovers. The sin is fornication (intimate relations with the kings of the inhabited earth). These may be vassal kings absorbed by the Roman Empire (Common Market). And with the favour of Rome, accepting her vices and idolatry.

A Harlot City

In verse three we need to remember verses one, eleven and fifteen for her dominion. Verse four has her attire and sins. Names of blasphemy cover the whole body of the beast upon which the woman sits (the harlot city, Rome). In verse five we have her name and in verse six her drunkenness. Roman harlots wore a label with their names on their brows. The name "Babylon" is to be interpreted mystically or spiritually for Rome. She is drunk with the blood of the martyrs.

A Mystical Person

In verse seven we note the promise of an explanation of the whore and beast. Then in verse eight we look at the beast. Verse eight shows a picture of the beast which the woman is riding – but no longer just the empire, but one of the emperors who died. He is going to come to life again. Time will show who that may be.

The Area

Verses 9-10 show the seven heads, and an explanation of the heads as seven mountains (hills) on which the woman sits and the seven kings in the Old Roman apostate Empire. In verse eleven we have the beast (the eighth kingdom ruled by the antichrist). In verse twelve we see the ten horns that are ten kingdoms presided over by the antichrist, in the Old Roman Empire. In verses 13-14 the ten kings will agree to give their kingdoms to help the antichrist (but continue as kings under him). The antichrist and the kings shall make war with the Lamb and shall be overcome and the Lamb's followers shall be "called and chosen and faithful" and the Lamb shall be known as "Lord of lords and King of kings." In verse fifteen the waters are the many people under the kings who hate the whore and make her desolate. In verses 16-17 the antichrist and the ten kings turn on the whore (city), perhaps in the middle of the seventieth week, so that the beast can rule the last three and a half years alone. Then in verse eighteen we are told that the woman is a city that reigns at that time over the ten kings as a religious centre.

The City

Now let us go back and look at certain facts. Our eyes and minds are, in our day, drawn away from the Roman church and its influence in and upon the world. Yet it would seem evident from verse nine that the woman (city) is apostate (worldly), and lies on seven mountains. Rome is the one city on seven mountains (hills). Here, then, you have the Babylonian system in the city of Rome. And, in our day, we must not ignore the fact that the World Council of Churches may also play a part in this scenario. The overthrow comes quickly (in one hour) (18:19). Destruction may come quickly as in Sodom and Gomorrah. The iniquity of Babylon lay in the fact that she martyred the saints.

Babylon

Again, the name Babylon (vs. 5), comes from the city of Babel (confusion). Genesis 10:8-10 says: "And Cush begat Nimrod; he began to be a mighty one in the earth. He was a mighty hunter before the Lord: wherefore it is said, Even as Nimrod the mighty hunter before the Lord. And the beginning of his kingdom was Babel... in the land of Shinar." She is the mystery of Satan. It was this Babylonian cult that is here in question; which later became the Roman system. It became a mystical Brotherhood which included Babylonians, (Arabs), Assyrians and Egyptians. Here we have a priest whose word is law. We are told that when Attalus, the Pontiff of Pergamos died in 133 B.C., he bequeathed the Headship of the Babylonian priesthood to Rome and thus Rome and Babylon came under one religious system.

The Founder

The founder of Babel was Nimrod (Gen. 10). Nimrod was a grandson of Ham, the unworthy son of Noah. His name means swarthy or darkened. Shem was dusky and Japheth means fair. Ham begat a son named Cush, the dark one, and he became the father of Nimrod. Cush is Ethiopia, Phut is Libya, Mizraim is Egypt and Canaan is Palestine. The wife of Nimrod was Samiramus and she was the high priestess of idolatry. She had a son whom she declared was miraculously conceived and the people received him as the "deliverer." This was Tammuz against whom Ezekiel protested in 8:14. "Then he brought me to the door of the gate of the Lord's house which was toward the north; and, behold, there sat women weeping for Tammuz." Here, then, begins the "mother and child" idolatry. It is the oldest or first known idolatry originated by Satan. It is Satan's effort to delude mankind so they would not recognize the "true Seed of the woman in the fullness of time." From Babylon this idea spread to Egypt as Iris and Horus; in Greece as Aphrodite and Eros; in Italy it was Venus and Cupid.

Mystery Religion

From this mystery religion Abraham was called out. Jezebel, the wife of Israel's king Ahab, grafted this religion unto the religion of Israel. Eventually, however, Rome likely became the home of Babylonianism. Mitres was shaped like the head of a fish in honour of Dagon, the fish god. The name "Pontifex-Maximum" was used until the time of Constantine, the Roman emperor who leaned toward and made Christianity the accepted religion. Pontifex means "a member of the principal college of priests in Rome" and "maximum" means "the head of the college" (by a comment of Pentecost (Things to Come) on The Two Babylons by Hislop).

Easter

Under Damasus, as chief Pontiff, the worship of the virgin Mary was set up, in A.D. 381. Easter, too, is not a Christian name. Easter comes from the Teutonic goddess to whom sacrifice was offered in April. So the name was transferred to the paschal lamb or feast. There is no trace of Easter celebration in the New Testament, although there may be a trace of Easter in 1 Corinthians 5:7-8. In Acts 12:4 the Greek has "Passover" for "Easter." We celebrate Easter as a feast for the true paschal Lamb who arose from the dead. (Read a write-up in an encyclopedia.)

Wrong Terms

The "Rosary" and even the sign of the cross may be of pagan origin. The sign of the cross may come from the letter T of the name Tammuz, a Babylonian leader. Also celibacy and the order of monks and nuns have no warrant from Scripture. One needs to consider the "Vestal Virgins" of the Greeks on the Acropolis. As for Lent, Passion would be a better word. The idea of the suffering of Christ is represented in such a word as passion. (Hislop, *The Two Babylons*). One also contemplates the mysteries of Baptismal regeneration, Transubstantiation, Holy water, candles, pictures, works, purgatory, images, etc. In Revelation 17:4 the woman (city) is arrayed in purple and scarlet and precious stones and gold. If one has visited St. Peter's cathedral, one has been impressed with all the foregoing. And in Rome the Christians were martyred; the catacombs attest to that. Verse six shows this to be true. And the apostate world church may have a part in this. All worldly religion will have a part in Babylon's system. Jeremiah may have had a revelation of this when he prophesied of the fall of Babylon. Jeremiah 51:6 says: "Flee out of the midst of Babylon, and deliver every man his soul: be not cut off in her iniquity; for this is the time of the Lord's vengeance; he will render unto her a recompence."

A Reference to the Common Market

The beast, we said, is the leader of the Roman leadership of the Common Market or ten kings. There are seven kings (vs. 10). We must note that when the antichrist (beast) comes, he plucks out three of the ten and he is the eighth (vs. 11). Five are fallen. The sixth, who reigned when John wrote, was Domitian. The seventh may yet come before the antichrist takes over. (He will rule only a short while (vs. 10)). The eighth is the beast. He will rule over the ten kings (federation). These array themselves against the Lamb (Lord) and shall be overcome. But the beast and kings (federation) shall hate the whore (city) and shall destroy her, so that God's will, which He has put in their hearts, be done. In all of this we must not dismiss the might of the Arab world which will certainly also have a part in this great conflict.

Political Babylon

The Doom of Babylon

In chapter eighteen we have the indictment of Babylon (vs. 1-3). It is not the angel of Revelation 17:1 who announces the doom of Babylon but another angel. He comes from the presence of heaven and sheds forth a broad belt of light across the dark earth. Babylon was a literal city and the center of pagan worship. It had eight towers, we are told, each seventy-five feet high; rising one upon the other to a height of six hundred and sixty feet. The sacred utensils in it were valued at a very high price. The city had hanging gardens and it was one of the seven wonders of the world. Its history goes back to about 4200 B.C., and a high level of culture was present.

Babylon and the Revived Roman Empire

We are dealing with political Babylon here which is the beast's confederated empire, the last form of Gentile world-dominion. It may be that

Babylon (Arab world) and Rome have the same confederated systems which will play a great part in the last days of the tribulation. In Rome no prophets of Old Testament times were slain. But what will transpire under the destruction of political Babylon, remains to be unfolded.

The Harlot and Her Influence

In chapter 17:1, one of the seven angels with the seven vials showed John the harlot. In chapter 21:9, the same angel showed John the Bride of Christ. What a difference the new birth accomplishes. Yet, this Babylon (political), had a tremendous influence on the kings and nations.

Babylon's Verdict

In verses 4-8 we have the verdict on Babylon. She has been the chief center of demon operations and a commercial center for all. In verse four Christ calls all who are still listening to "come out of her, my people." Even under this revived Roman Empire and under this confederacy, there are those who still side with Christ. Could Christ, even today, be calling to Christians to leave the ecumenical movements and baptismal regeneration and worldly and satanic religions? This may be Love's Final Solution. At this late hour Christ is still being patient and loving to those who come out of a sin-sick world. So came the call to Abraham and Lot, and Ephesians 5:11 says: "And have no fellowship with the unfruitful works of darkness, but rather reprove them." Sins have a way of multiplying and so, God observing the increase of wrong doing, decides to requite her in double measure the punishment coming to her.

The Loss

Verse seven shows her as a personified queen and chief of all cities. Isaiah 47:5,7 reads: "Sit thou silent, and get thee into darkness, O daughter of the Chaldeans; for thou shalt no more be called, The lady of kingdoms. And thou saidst, I shall be a lady for ever: so that thou didst not lay these things to thy heart, neither didst remember the latter end of it." For her assertion of being "a queen" and shall see no sorrow, she shall no more be called "the lady of kingdoms," but shall in a moment see the loss of all.

Babylon's Plagues

Verse eight shows her four plagues. Death, mourning, famine and she shall be burned with fire. It is the Lord who judges her and shows that Babylon is destroyed in the presence of the kings and is lamented by them (vs. 9-10). The lamentation is first of all, by the governmental world (kings) and also by the commercial world (vs. 11-16).

The Great Lament

Here is a list of articles of commerce: Gold, silver, pearls, purple, scarlet, odours, wine, oil, wheat, beasts, sheep, horses, chariots, slaves, fruits, silk, precious stones, fine linen, thyine wood (kind of African tree-precious wood), vessels of ivory, wood, brass, iron, marble, cinnamon, ointments, frankincense, dainty things and goodly things and fine flour. They also lament over her for the maritime world. It shows that travellers of many places are here visiting and trading in the city. Antichrist will have control of great riches in the last days. No wonder the merchants will weep and mourn for the city.

The Final Blow

Commercialism receives here its final blow. It is the cause of evil in man. It distributes wealth, it creates poverty, it causes prices to fluctuate by trade. The stock or market exchange of 1929 caused a depression. Commercialism also causes universal greed and produces spiritual darkness and deadness. Just as Nero's delight in the burning of Rome, so here the mourning for the burning of the revived Roman Empire.

Rejoicing

In verse twenty heaven is to rejoice three times:

1. When Satan is cast out (12:12).
2. When Babylon is destroyed (18:20).
3. When the marriage of the Lamb is come (19:7).

Mourning and Rejoicing

While the kings and merchants mourn and wail the destruction of the city, heaven and apostles and prophets are to rejoice, for God has avenged them on the idolatry of the city. There shall be no more the voice of harpers and musicians; of pipers and trumpeters; of craftsman and the sound of the millstone. There shall not be heard the voice of the bridegroom and of the bride.

Babylon's Weaknesses

Here are some causes for the doom of Babylon (vs. 21-24).

1. *Pride.* Isaiah 13:19 says: "And Babylon, the *glory* of kingdoms, the beauty of the Chaldees' excellency, shall be as when God overthrew Sodom and Gomorrah."

2. *Oppression of Israel.* Isaiah 13:1 says: "The *burden* of Babylon, which Isaiah the son of Amos did see."

3. *Pleasures/luxuries.* Isaiah 47:1,8 says: "Come down, and sit in the dust, o virgin daughter of Babylon.... Therefore hear now this, thou that art given to pleasures."

4. *Idol worship.* Jeremiah 50:2 says: "Declare ye among the nations, and publish, and set up a standard; publish and conceal not: say, Babylon is taken, Bel is confounded, Merodach is broken in pieces; her idols are confounded, her images are broken in pieces."

5. *Fornication* (Rev. 18:3-9).

6. *Spiritism* (Rev. 18:2).

7. *Sorceries.* Isaiah 47:12 says: "Stand now with thine enchantments, and with the multitude of thy sorceries, wherein thou hast laboured from thy youth."

8. *Martyrdom of saints and prophets* (Rev. 18:6,24).

And verse twenty-four shows that she will be held responsible for many, many deaths. Rome "butchered to make a Roman holiday (Dill, *Roman*

Society, p. 242) not merely gladiators, but prophets and saints from Nero's massacre A.D. 64 to Domitian and beyond.

Destruction

At this time the earthquake through the action of the angel, destroys commercial Babylon (vs. 21). This ends the wrath of God begun under the sixth seal in the first of three and a half years of Daniel's seventieth week in Revelation 6:12-17.

REVELATION 19

The Four Alleluias

When Babylon, the apostate worldly church, in its political aims, is finally overthrown, then the righteous assembly can rejoice. And it does so with four "Alleluias" (vs. 1,3,4,6). After the climax of chapter 18, Revelation 19:1 speaks of "much people in heaven" (Greek: *a great crowd*), proving they have been caught up before. Consider, all the saints of all time, in a vast throng, expressing their "praise to Jehovah," for that is what the word means. Let us now look at the events between the rapture and the Revelation in relation to the idea of "much people in heaven."

Concerning the Rapture

1. Here we have the presentation before God. Ephesians 5:27 says: "That he might present it to himself a glorious Church, not having spot, or wrinkle, or any such thing: but that it should be holy and without blemish."

2. The saints are declared blameless. 1 Thessalonians 3:13a says: "To the end he may stablish your hearts unblameable in holiness before

God, even our Father, at the coming of our Lord Jesus Christ, *with* all his saints."

3. There will be a settlement in mansions. John 14:1-3 says: "Let not your heart be troubled: ye believe in God, believe also in me. In my Father's house are many mansions: if it were not so, I would have told you. I go to prepare a place for you. And if I go and prepare a place for you, I will come again, and receive you unto myself: that where I am, there ye may be also."

4. Then will occur also the judgment of the believer's works. 2 Corinthians 5:10 says: "For we must all appear before the judgment seat of Christ; that everyone may receive the things done in his body, according to that he hath done, whether it be good or bad."

5. There will be regular worship (Rev. 19:1-9).

6. The routine of living shall be regulated. Luke 22:30 says: "And I appoint unto you a kingdom, as my Father hath appointed unto me; That ye may eat and drink at my table in my kingdom, and sit on thrones judging the twelve tribes of Israel."

7. There will be the marriage of the Lamb (Rev. 19:1-9).

8. Then will be the preparation for the second Advent, the battle of Armageddon and the establishment of a millennial government (Rev. 19:11-21; Zech. 14).

The word "Alleluia" also may be expressed as the Hebrew "Hallelu-Jah" (Praise ye Jah) or "praise ye the Lord." This is the cry of victory (vs. 6).

Facts About Christ

At this point we must state some facts about Christ. The Greek aorist tense is used in verse six for "the Lord God omnipotent reigneth." It denotes "completed actions." Hebrews 12:22-23: "But ye are come... to the general assembly and church of the firstborn, which are written in heaven, and to God the Judge of all, and to the spirits of just men made perfect."

1. Christ rides a white horse (Rev. 19:11).

2. He comes from heaven (vs. 11).

3. He is called faithful (vs. 11).

4. He is called true (vs. 11).

5. He makes war in righteousness (vs. 11).

6. He judges in righteousness (vs. 11).

7. His eyes are as flames of fire (vs. 12).

8. He has many crowns on His head (vs. 12).

9. His body is clothed with a vesture dipped in blood (vs. 13).

10. He has three names:

    a. A name that no one knows (vs. 12).

    b. The Word of God (vs. 13).

    c. King of kings and Lord of lords (vs. 16).

11. He is commander-in-chief of all the armies of heaven (vs. 14).

12. Out of His mouth goes a sharp sword to smite the nations (vs. 15).

13. He will rule the nations with a rod of iron (vs. 15).

14. He will tread the winepress of the fierceness of the wrath of God (vs. 15).

15. He will conquer antichrist at Armageddon (vs. 19-21). Joel 3:12 says: "Let the heathen be wakened, and come up to the valley of Jehoshaphat: for there will I sit to judge all the heathen round about."

16. He will reign on earth 1000 years (Rev. 20:1-10).

17. He and the Father will be the eternal sanctuary (Rev. 20:1-10).

18. He and the Father will be the eternal light (Rev. 21:23).

19. He will have a throne on the right hand of God forever (Rev. 22:1).

20. He will reign after all enemies are put down (Rev. 22:5). Daniel 7:13-14 says: "I saw in the night visions, and, behold, one like the Son of man came with the clouds of heaven, and came to the Ancient of days, and they brought him near before him. And there was given him dominion and glory, and a kingdom, that all people, nations, and languages, should serve him: his dominion is an everlasting dominion, which shall not pass away, and his kingdom that which shall not be destroyed."

Praise to the Godhead

It is the angel who summons all the servants of God to join in the antiphonal praise to God. It is an innumerable multitude of the redeemed. God became king in fullness of power on earth with the fall of the world power. In the Old Testament God is the Bridegroom of Israel. Hosea 2:16a reads: "And it shall be at that day, saith the Lord, that thou shalt call me Ishi (husband) and shalt call me no more Baali" (master). In the New Testament Christ is the Bridegroom of the Church. 2 Corinthians 11:2 says: "For I am jealous over you with godly jealousy: for I have espoused you to one husband, that I may present you as a chaste virgin to Christ." Three metaphors of women appear in Revelation: The Mother in chapter twelve; the Harlot in chapter seventeen and the Bride of Christ in chapter nineteen. The bridal dress is a gift from Christ (vs. 8).

The Marriage of the Lamb

Then, in verse seven, we have the "Marriage of the Lamb," to which the Ages have looked. Again, the Greek aorist tense denotes completed action. The Song of Solomon describes a bride seeking her lover. So the Church escapes her captivity in this world and is united to her Lover, the Lord. Also, a comparison of this union, in the Old Testament, is the meeting of Isaac and Rebekah. In the New Testament, the story of the Ten Virgins relates to this event, as does also the events of Matthew 22:1-10, the marriage of the King's son.

"And Jesus answered and spake unto them again by parables, and said, The kingdom of heaven is like unto a certain king, which made a marriage for his son, And sent forth his servants to call them that were bidden to the wedding: and they would not come. Again, he sent forth other servants, saying, tell them which are bidden, behold, I

have prepared my dinner; my oxen and my fatlings are killed, and all things are ready: come unto the marriage.

"But they made light of it, and went their ways, one to his farm, another to his merchandise: And the remnant took his servants, and entreated them spitefully, and slew them. But when the king heard thereof, he was wroth: and he sent forth his armies, and destroyed those murderers, and burnt up their city. Then saith he to his servants, the wedding is ready, but they which were bidden, were not worthy. Go ye therefore into the highways, and as many as ye shall find, bid to the marriage. So those servants went out into the highways and gathered together all as many as they found, both bad and good: and the wedding was furnished with guests."

The man without a wedding garment was cast into outer darkness, "For many are called, but few are chosen."

This is the marriage of the Lamb and not so much that of the Bride. It is the plan of God for His Son, arranged before the foundation of the world" (Eph. 1:4). And Revelation 19:9 says: "And he saith unto me, Write, Blessed are they which are called unto the marriage supper of the Lamb. And he saith unto me, These are the true sayings of God."

The Word Made Flesh

Therefore Jesus had to come into the flesh since the Bride is of human origin. Otherwise they would have had dissimilar natures. But Jesus took on human nature and changed it into a spiritual nature in which the Holy Spirit resides. The espousal could not be before the foundation of the world. The plan was made then and the act performed in Revelation nineteen, in God's time. We said, Jesus had to assume humanity to redeem humans, but there was infinitely more. His body was resurrected from the dead, for death could not hold Him. In like manner, the redeemed, so that there might be similarity as John, the apostle, says: "We shall be like Him," when He appears (1 John 3:2). Our destiny, therefore, is a similarity of nature and being because He saved us. Here, then, is the betrothal, the blessed unity. We are one in having a transformed body and this is our glory. Also, "to be conformed to the image of His Son." Romans 8:29 says: "For whom he did foreknow, he also did predestinate to be conformed to the image of his Son, that he might be the firstborn among many brethren."

The Saints

The marriage takes place in heaven where the Bridegroom is with His Bride (vs. 6). This marriage occurs after the judgment of rewards of crowns and before Christ appears visibly *with* His saints. Colossians 3:4 says: "When Christ, who is our life, shall appear, then shall ye also appear with him in glory." And 1 Thessalonians 3:13 says: "To the end he may stablish your hearts unblameable in holiness before God, even our Father, at the coming of our Lord Jesus Christ *with* all his saints." And Jude 14 says: "And Enoch also, the seventh from Adam, prophesied of these, saying, Behold, the Lord cometh *with* ten thousands of his saints."

The Church is the Bride of Jesus. Israel is the wife of God. Hosea 2:16 says: "And it shall be at that day, saith the Lord, that thou shalt call me Ishi (my husband); and shalt call me no more Baali (my master)."

Israel will be taken back as a wife, not a virgin, for the Church is a virgin (2 Cor. 11:2). The Bridegroom is Christ. John the Baptist spoke of Jesus as the Bridegroom and he as the friend (John 3:29). And Jesus referred to Himself as the Bridegroom. Matthew 9:15 says: "And Jesus said unto them, Can the children of the bridechamber mourn, as long as the Bridegroom is with them? but the days will come, when the bridegroom shall be taken from them, and then shall they fast."

The Bride's Dress

The Bride is clothed in fine linen and this represents the righteousness of saints. The word "righteousness," in verse eight, is in the Greek in the plural form, as "righteousnesses" or "righteous deeds" of the saints. It is not the righteousness imputed through Christ. This, then, is after the judgment seat of Christ. It is the *righteous position* we have *after* our works have been judged.

The Marriage Supper

In verse nine, John is asked to write because "these are the true sayings of God." The verse speaks about the marriage supper. This would seem to be after the marriage. Verse nine makes it plain that many are called (invited) to this supper. No bride needs an invitation to her wedding. The guests may be Old Testament saints and friends like John the Baptist. Hebrews 12:23 says: "But ye are come... to the general assembly and church of the firstborn, which are written in heaven, and to God, the Judge of all, and to the spirits of just men made perfect," and perhaps tribulation saints. Angels are the spectators. Ephesians 1:9-10 speaks about the Fullness of Times, which we must consider under "the fullness of Gentiles" (Rom. 11:25-27); and "the Times of the Gentiles," of Luke 21:24. Romans 11:25-27 says: "For I would not, brethren, that ye should be ignorant of this mystery, lest ye should be wise in your own conceits; that blindness *in part* happened to Israel, until the *fullness of the Gentiles* be come in. And so all Israel shall be saved: as it is written, There shall come out of Sion the Deliverer, and shall turn away ungodliness from Jacob: For this is my covenant unto them, when I shall take away their sins." And Luke 21:24 says: "And they shall fall by the edge of the sword, and shall be led away captive into all nations; and Jerusalem shall be trodden down of the Gentiles, until the *times of the Gentiles* be fulfilled." The fullness of the Gentiles refers to those of the Gentiles who partake of the grace of God and accept the Lord Jesus as Saviour and belong to the Church of Christ. The times of the Gentiles refers to the Gentile nations from beginning to the end of history in the battle of Armageddon of Revelation 19. Here, then, the welfare of Israel falls under the *times of the Gentiles.*

This the seventh and last of the ordered ages which condition human life on earth, is identified with the Kingdom covenanted to David, and gathers into itself under Christ all past times. Zechariah 12:8 says: "In that day shall the Lord defend the inhabitants of Jerusalem; and he that is feeble among them at that day shall be as David; and the house of David shall be as God, as the angel of the Lord before them."

Misrule Ends With Christ

1. The time of oppression and misrule ends by Christ taking His Kingdom. Isaiah 11:1-4a says: "And there shall come forth a rod out of the stem of Jesse, and a Branch shall grow out of his roots: and the spirit of the Lord shall rest upon Him, the spirit of wisdom and understanding, the spirit of counsel and might, the spirit of knowledge and of the fear of the Lord... but with righteousness shall He judge the poor, and reprove with equity for the meek of the earth: and he shall smite the earth with the rod of his mouth, and with the breath of his lips shall He slay the wicked."

2. The time of testimony and forbearance ends in judgment. Matthew 25:34-35: "Then shall the King say unto them on his right hand, Come, ye blessed of my Father, inherit the kingdom prepared for you from the foundation of the world; For I was an hungred, and ye gave me meat: I was thirsty, and ye gave me drink: I was a stranger, and ye took me in."

3. The time of toil ends in rest and reward. 2 Thessalonians 1:6 says: "Seeing it is a righteous thing with God to recompense tribulation

to them that trouble you: and to you who are troubled rest with us."

4. The time of suffering ends in glory. Romans 8:18 says: "For I reckon that the sufferings of this present time are not worthy to be compared with the glory which shall be revealed in us."

5. The time of Israel's blindness and chastisement ends in restoration and conversion. Romans 11:25 reads: "For I would not, brethren, that ye should be ignorant of this mystery, lest ye should be wise in your own conceits; that blindness in part is happened to Israel, until the fullness of the Gentiles be come in."

6. The times of the Gentiles end in the smiting of the Image and the setting up of the Kingdom of heaven. Daniel 2:34-35b says: "Thou sawest till that a stone was cut out without hands, which smote the image upon his feet that were of iron and clay, and brake them to pieces... and the stone that smote the image became a great mountain, and filled the whole earth."

7. The time of creation's thraldom ends in deliverance at the manifestation of the sons of God. Isaiah 11:6-8 says: "The wolf also shall dwell with the lamb, and the leopard shall lie down with the kid; and the calf and the young lion and the fatling together; and a little child shall lead them. And the cow and the bear shall feed; their young ones shall lie down together; and the lion shall eat straw like the ox. And the sucking child shall play on the hole of the asp, and the weaned child shall put his hand on the cockatrice den."

Worship Must Be to God

In this glorious consummation, John was tempted to worship an angel. The angel refuses worship from John because all Christians are fellow-servants as Christ taught (Matt. 18:28ff). Angels are God's servants also (Heb. 1:4-14). And in verse ten, the possession of the prophetic spirit shows itself in witness to Jesus.

The Second Coming of Christ

In Revelation 19:11-16 we have, then, the visible second coming of Christ as the Faithful and True, who has kept His Promise that He would come again. He is the King of kings and Lord of lords. This is the day of wrath. It is not the Great White Throne Judgment. The Day of Wrath and the Great White Throne Judgment are separated by one thousand years. This here is Armageddon which gets things cleared up for the one thousand year's reign of Christ.

The rider of verse eleven is different from the rider in Revelation 6:2. Here it is the Messiah who is the Warrior, as is made plain by "Faithful and True." His eyes are as a flame of fire and He wears many crowns (diadems) because He is the King of kings. The day of wrath is the pent-up divine outburst of indignation of outraged holiness, love and truth. This is Love's final solution for evil and sin. It is the answer to the prayers of His saints. God makes now His power known. His clothes were as if dipped in blood. Never are we to forget His love for mankind in the sacrifice He made. Permitted evil will now finally be judged. Christ and His vast army execute judgment. Psalm 2:9 says: "Thou shalt break them with a rod of iron; Thou shalt dash them in pieces like a potter's vessel." And Psalm 2:12 says: "Kiss the Son, lest he be angry, and ye perish from the way, when His wrath is kindled but a little. Blessed are all they that put their trust in Him." Jesus fights the battle, not by sword, but by Word of mouth. By that sword He smites the nations. Enoch of old prophesied of this battle. Jude 14 says: "And Enoch also, the seventh from Adam, prophesied of these, saying, Behold, the Lord cometh with ten thousands of his saints." There is an army on horses (vs. 14), as in the time of Elijah. 2 Kings 2:11b says: "there appeared a chariot of fire, and horses of fire." And 2 Kings 6:17 says: "And Elisha prayed, and said, Lord, I pray thee, open his eyes, that he may see. And the Lord opened the eyes of the young man; and he saw: and, behold, the mountain was full of horses and chariots of fire round about Elisha." It would seem that heaven is not so far distant as we think. All that is necessary is the opening of eyes. So often our eyes are holden, so we cannot see the glory of heaven about us. As the eyes of the Emmaus disciples, which were held so they knew not Jesus, until their eyes were opened (Luke 24:13-34). The writer, also, of Hebrews says that we are surrounded by so great a cloud of witnesses. Hebrews 12:1 says: "Wherefore seeing we also are compassed about with so great a *cloud* of witnesses, let us lay aside every weight, and the sin which doth so easily beset us, and let us run with patience the race that is set before us." If only our eyes could be opened to see the glory of such a cloud. This is also the promise made to the Over-comers of the Thyatiran church period – to reign with Him in the thousand year reign.

Jesus is Himself the final and perfect revelation of God to men (vs. 13). It is now the day of vengeance because men would not accept that Word of God. Isaiah 63:1-4 says: "Who is this that cometh from Edom, with dyed garments from Bozrah? this that is glorious in his apparel, travelling in the greatness of his strength: I that speak in righteousness, mighty to Save. Wherefore art thou red in thine apparel, and thy garments like him that treadeth in the winefat? I have trodden the winepress alone; and of the people there was none with me: for I will tread them in mine anger, and trample them in my fury; and their blood shall be sprinkled upon my garments, and I will stain all my garment, For the day of vengeance is in my heart, and the year of my redeemed is come."

The Supper of the Great God

There is no mercy or forgiveness, rather wrath and punishment. Here are gathered all the kings and rulers and the fowls are invited to come to the supper of the great God. It is the battle of Armageddon. The beast (antichrist) and the False Prophet are cast into the lake of fire (vs. 20). The word "alive" shows them in human form. This place is also "Gehenna." Matthew 10:28 says: "And fear not them which kill the body, but are not able to kill the soul: but rather fear him which is able to destroy (separation, punishment, death) both soul and body in hell" (gehenna). And the beast and false prophet are still there when Satan is cast into the lake of fire after one thousand years (Rev. 20:10). And concerning the "fire," let us leave that description and meaning as the Word of God describes it. Jude refers to the angels which kept not their first estate, as kept under "chains of darkness" until the great day and speaks of Sodom and Gomorrah as suffering the vengeance of eternal fire. It is all in God's plan and hands.

A Great Burial

This battle is described in the Old Testament by the prophet Ezekiel in chapter 39:11-12a. "And it shall come to pass in that day, that I will give unto Gog a place there of graves in Israel, the valley of the passengers on the east of the sea... and there shall they bury Gog and all his multitude... and seven months shall the house of Israel be burying of them, that they may cleanse the land." That same chapter says that Israel will be busy seven months burying the dead. This is a bold and powerful picture of the battlefield after the victory of the Messiah, a sacrificial feast spread on God's table for all the vultures of the sky. Here, also, will be fulfilled the words of Matthew 24:28, "For wheresoever the carcass is, there will the eagles be gathered together." The meaning is, where Israel is situated, the nations will be gathered. Regarding the battle of Armageddon, we note these facts:

Armageddon

1. *The place.* Zechariah 14:1a-2a says: "Behold the day of the Lord cometh.... For I will gather all nations against Jerusalem to battle." Zechariah names the place as Jerusalem.

2. *The time* – Pre-millennial.

   1. At the second advent to deliver the Jews from antichrist (vs. 11-21).
   2. After the great tribulation (vs. 11-21).
   3. After the marriage supper of the Lamb (19:1-21).
   4. When Jerusalem is surrounded by the armies of all nations under the antichrist (vs. 19-21; Zech. 14:1-15).
   5. Just before the millennium (vs. 11-21).
   6. At the end of this age of grace (vs. 11-21).
   7. When the first resurrection is completed (20:6).
   8. At the time Satan is bound (19:11-20).
   9. When Israel has been in the wilderness 3 1/2 years (11:1-3).
   10. When the seals, trumpets and vials are fulfilled (16:17-21).
   11. One thousand years before the new heavens and new earth (19:11-20).

3. *The combatants.* It will be Christ and the heavenly armies against Satan and his armies under antichrist (19:17-19). Daniel 7:19-27, says: "Then I would know the truth of the fourth beast, which was diverse from all the others, exceeding dreadful, whose teeth were of iron, and his nails of brass; which devoured, brake in pieces, and stamped the residue with his feet. And of the ten horns that were in his head, and of the other which came up, and before whom three fell: even of that horn that had eyes, and a mouth that spake very great

things, whose look was more stout than his fellows. I beheld, and the same horn made war with the saints, and prevailed against them; Until the Ancient of days came, and judgment was given to the saints of the most High; and the time came that the saints possessed the kingdom. Thus he said, The fourth beast shall be the *fourth* kingdom upon the earth, which shall be diverse from all kingdoms, and shall devour the whole earth, and shall tread it down, and break it in pieces. And the ten horns out of this kingdom are ten kings that shall arise; and another shall rise after them; and he shall be diverse from the first, and he shall subdue three kings. And he shall speak great words against the most High, and shall wear out the saints of the most High, and think to change times and laws; and they shall be given into his hand, until a time and times and the dividing of time. But the judgment shall sit, and they shall take away his dominion, to consume and to destroy it unto the end. And the kingdom and dominion, and the greatness of the kingdom under the whole heaven, shall be given to the people of the saints of the most High, whose kingdom is an everlasting kingdom, and all dominions shall serve and obey him."

4. *The purpose of Armageddon.* Satan is trying to stop Christ from taking over the earth (Rev. 19:19-21). And it is the end of false statecraft and the end of false priestcraft (Swete).

The Millennium

Names

In Revelation 20:1-3 we see the devil with four names: Dragon, Serpent, Devil and Satan. Each of these names has its own connotation. The word "dragon" refers back to serpent as in the garden of Eden where the serpent (deceiver) is used. The word "serpent" is known as an emblem of cunning or hypocrite. The word "devil" is associated with slander and accusing falsely. He is the false accuser. The word "Satan" shows the prince of demons; the author of evil. He incites to apostasy from God and to sin. He also afflicts with diseases. Whatever the chain is we cannot say, but it may denote the fact that it be a curtailing of the ability of Satan to incite to apostasy. And he is cast into the abyss where he is unable to deceive the nations for a period of a thousand years. The Greek for "abyss" denotes an unbounded, bottomless abode, the abode of demons. Jude 6 speaks of chains of darkness in which the angels, who kept not their first estate, are kept.

Satan Bound

The angel binds Satan with this chain for one thousand years and casts him in the deep pit. This is not the lake of fire into which all the ungodly are cast later. This abyss is also not an influence for you cannot cast or bind an influence or a principle of evil, but you can bind a person.

The First Resurrection

Verses 4-6 show us the first resurrection. Here are two companies of believers:

1. Those upon "thrones." 1 Thessalonians 4:16 notes that those in Christ shall be raised together (the dead and the living) to meet the Lord in the air and here they are giving judgment together with Christ. 1 Corinthians 6:2,3 says: "Do ye not know that the saints shall judge the world? And if the world shall be judged by you, are ye unworthy to judge the smallest matters? Know ye not that we shall judge angels?"

2. The second company are those who came out of the tribulation period. They had not worshiped the beast nor the image nor received his mark. They seem to be the gleanings of the harvest.

The rest of the dead, in verse five, are the wicked dead who are mentioned in verse twelve.

This also proves that there can be not just one final resurrection where both the righteous and wicked are raised. It is clear that there is a time space of one thousand years between the two. Note also the words in verse four, "and they lived and reigned with Christ a thousand years." This is the direct administration of divine government on earth for one thousand years, of Christ and His Church. The name "millennium" is from the Latin "mille" (1000) and "annum" (year). A better word that Jesus used is "kingdom." It is the stone kingdom mentioned by Daniel, that follows the four other kingdoms. Daniel 2:44-45 says: "And in the days of these kings shall the God of heaven set up a kingdom, which shall never be destroyed: and the kingdom shall not be left to other people, but it shall break in pieces and consume all these kingdoms, and it shall stand forever. Forasmuch as thou sawest that the stone was cut out of the mountain without hands, and that it braek in pieces the iron, the brass, the clay, the silver, and the gold: the great God hath made known to the king what shall come to pass hereafter." Daniel 7 names the kingdoms: Babylon, Media-Persia, Greece and Rome. This earthly kingdom is visible (Matt. 25:31-34). Let us now look at the scriptural view of the millennium. Some of these are mentioned by J. Dwight Pentecost in "Things to Come" and from other commentaries.

Covenants

This one thousand year reign of Christ will see the fulfillment of all the covenants that God made with Israel.

A. *The Abrahamic covenant.* Micah 7:20 says: "Thou wilt perform the truth to Jacob, and the mercy to Abraham, which thou hast sworn unto our fathers from the days of old." Other

Scriptures that deal with this truth are: Isa. 10:21-22; Jer. 30:22; Ezek. 34:24; Zech. 13:9.

B. *The Davidic covenant.* Jeremiah 23:5 says: "Behold the days come, saith the Lord, that I will raise unto David a righteous Branch, and a king shall reign and prosper, and shall execute judgment and justice in the earth." Other Scriptures are: Isa. 11:1,2; Ezek. 34:23-25; Hos. 3:5.

C. *The Palestinian covenant.* Isaiah 11:11-12 says: "And it shall come to pass in that day, that the Lord shall set his hand again the second time to recover the remnant of his people, which shall be left, from Assyria, and from Egypt, and from Pathros, and from Cush, and from Elam, and from Shinar, and from Hamath, and from the islands of the sea. And he shall set up an ensign for the nations, and shall assemble the outcasts of Israel, and gather together the dispersed of Judah from the four corners of the earth." Other Scriptures are: Ezek. 16:60-63; Hos. 1:10-2:1; Micah 2:12.

D. *The new covenant – a new heart.* Ezekiel 11:19 says: "And I will give them one heart, and I will put a new spirit within you; and I will take the stony heart out of their flesh, and I will give them an heart of flesh." Other Scriptures are: Jer. 31:31-34; Rom. 11:26-29.

Names of Christ

Satan will be bound and removed from the scene so that temptation cannot test humanity. Let us look at the names ascribed to Christ in the millennium.

1. *The Branch.* Isaiah 4:2 says: "In that day shall the "branch" of the Lord be beautiful and glorious, and the fruit of the earth shall be excellent and comely for them that are escaped of Israel." Other Scriptures are: Jer. 23:5; Zech. 3:8-9.

2. *The Lord of Hosts.* Isaiah 24:23 says: "Then the moon shall be confounded, and the sun ashamed, when the Lord of hosts shall reign in mount Zion, and in Jerusalem, and before his ancients gloriously."

3. *Thy God.* Isaiah 52:7 says: "How beautiful upon the mountains are the feet of him that bringeth good tidings, that publisheth peace; that bringeth good tidings of good, that publisheth salvation; that saith unto Zion, Thy God reigneth!"

4. *The Ancient of days.* Daniel 7:13 says: "I saw in the night visions, and, beheld, one like the Son of Man came with the clouds of heaven, and came to the Ancient of days, and they brought him near before him."

5. *The Lord.* Micah 4:7 says: "And I will make her that halted a remnant, and her that was cast far off a strong nation: and the Lord shall reign over them in mount Zion from henceforth, even for ever."

6. *The Most High.* Daniel 7:22 says: "Until the Ancient of days came, and judgment was given to the saints of the Most High; and the time came that the saints possessed the kingdom."

7. *The Son of God.* Daniel 3:25 says: "He answered and said, Lo, I see four men loose, walking in the midst of the fire, and they have

no hurt; and the form of the fourth is like the Son of God."

8. *Jehovah.* Isaiah 2:3 says: "And many people shall go and say, Come ye, and let us go up to the mountain of the Lord (Jehovah), to the house of the God of Jacob, and he will teach us of his ways, and we will walk in his paths: for out of Zion shall go forth the law, and the word of the Lord (Jehovah) from Jerusalem."

9. *The Rod of Jesse.* Isaiah 11:1 says: "And there shall come forth a *rod* out of the stem of *Jesse*, and a branch shall grow out of his roots."

10. *The Son of Man.* Daniel 7:13a says: "I saw in the night visions, and, behold, one like the Son of man came with the clouds of heaven...."

11. *The Tender Plant.* Isaiah 53:2a says: "For he shall grow up before him as a tender plant, and as a root out of a dry ground."

12. *The King.* Isaiah 33:17a says: "Thine eyes shall see the King in his beauty."

13. *The Judge.* Isaiah 11:4a says: "But with right-eousness shall he judge the poor."

14. *The Lawgiver.* Isaiah 33:22 says: "For the Lord is our judge, the Lord is our Lawgiver, the Lord is our king; he will save us."

15. *Messiah the Prince.* Daniel 9:25a says: "Know therefore and understand, that from the going forth of the commandment to restore and to build Jerusalem unto the Messiah the Prince shall be seven weeks."

16. *Prince of princes.* Daniel 8:25b says: "He shall also stand up against the Prince of princes;

but he shall be broken without hand."

17. *The Redeemer.* Isaiah 59:20a says: "And the Redeemer shall come to Zion, and unto them that turn from transgression in Jacob, saith the Lord."

18. *The Sun of Righteousness.* Malachi 4:2a says: "But unto you that fear my name shall the Sun of righteousness arise with healing in his wings."

19. *The Wall Breaker.* Micah 2:13: "The breaker is come up before them; they have broken up, and have passed through the gate."

20. *The Shepherd.* Isaiah 40:11a: "He shall feed his flock like a shepherd."

21. *The Lord our Righteousness.* Jeremiah 23:6: "In his days Judah shall be saved, and Israel shall dwell safely: and this is his name whereby he shall be called, The Lord our Righteousness."

22. *The Stone.* Isaiah 28:16: "Therefore thus saith the Lord God, behold, I lay in Zion for a foundation a stone, a tried stone, a precious corner stone, a sure foundation."

23. *The Light.* Isaiah 60:1: "Arise, shine, for thy light is come, and the glory of the Lord is risen upon thee."

Jesus will be manifested as:

1. *The Son of Abraham.* In Matthew 1:1 we read, "The book of the generation of Jesus Christ, the Son of David, the Son of Abraham." Other Scriptures: Gen. 17:8; Gal. 3:16.

2. *The Son of David.* Luke 1:32 says: "He shall be great, and shall be called the Son of the Highest: and the Lord God shall give unto him the throne of his father David." Also Isa. 9:7.

3. *The Son of man.* Daniel 7:13 says: "I saw in the night visions, and, behold, one like the Son of man came with the clouds of heaven, and came to the Ancient of days, and they brought him near before him."

4. *Teacher.* Deuteronomy 18:15: "The Lord thy God will raise up unto thee a Prophet from the midst of thee, of thy brethren; unto him ye shall hearken."

5. *Lawgiver.* Isaiah 33:22: "For the Lord is our judge, the Lord is our lawgiver, the Lord is our King; he will save us."

The millennium will show Him in all His names, showing His humanity and His glory; His omniscience and omnipotence; His mercy and goodness; His holiness and truth. And Love's final solution.

Conditions in the Millennium

Let us now also look at the conditions existing in the millennium. There shall be "peace." Isaiah 60:18 says: "Violence shall no more be heard in thy land, wasting nor destruction within thy borders; but thou shalt call thy walls Salvation, and thy gates Praise." There shall be "Joy." Isaiah 60:15 says: "Whereas thou hast been forsaken and hated, so that no man went through thee, I will make thee an eternal excellency, a *joy* of many generations." There shall be "Holiness." Isaiah

61:10 says: "He hath covered me with the robe of righteousness." There shall be "glory." Isaiah 24:23 says: "Then the moon shall be confounded, and the sun ashamed, when the Lord of hosts shall reign in mount Zion, and in Jerusalem, and before his ancients gloriously." There shall be "comfort." Isaiah 12:1 says: "And in that day thou shalt say, O Lord, I will praise thee; though Thou wast angry with me, thine anger is turned away, and thou comfortedst me." There shall be "Justice." Isaiah 65:23 says: "They shall not labour in vain, nor bring forth for trouble; for they are the seed of the blessed of the Lord, and their offspring with them." There shall be "Full knowledge." Isaiah 11:9 says: "They shall not hurt nor destroy in all my holy mountain (kingdom): for the earth shall be full of the knowledge of the Lord, as the waters cover the sea." There shall be "The removal of the Curse." Isaiah 65:25 says: "The wolf and the lamb shall feed together, and the lion shall eat straw like the bullock: and dust shall be the serpents meat. They shall not hurt nor destroy in all my holy mountain, saith the Lord." With this removal one might include "changes" in the animal kingdom. Isaiah 11:6 says: "The wolf also shall dwell with the lamb; and the leopard shall lie down with the kid; and the calf and the young lion and the fatling together; and a little child shall lead them." "Sickness" will be removed. Ezekiel 34:16 says: "I will seek that which was lost... and will strengthen that which was sick." There will be "Freedom from oppression." Zechariah 9:11 says: "As for thee also, by the blood of thy covenant I have sent forth thy prisoners out of the pit wherein is no water." There is no Immaturity. Isaiah 65:20 says: "There shall be no more thence an infant of days, nor an old man that hath not filled his days: for the child shall die an hundred years old; but the sinner being an hundred years old shall be accursed." There will be reproduction by the living people. Jeremiah 30:20 says: "Their children also shall be as aforetime, and their congregation shall be established before me." There will be economic prosperity. Isaiah 65:21: "And they shall build houses, and inhabit them; and they shall plant vineyards, and eat the fruit of them." Light shall be changed. Isaiah 60:19 says: "For the Lord shall be thy everlasting light." In the millennium will be "unified language." Zephaniah 3:9 says: "For then will I turn to the people a pure language, that they may all call upon the name of the Lord, to serve him with one consent." There will be "unified worship." Isaiah 66:23 says: "And it shall come to pass, that from one new moon to another, and from one Sabbath to another, shall all flesh come to worship before me, saith the Lord." There will be "the manifest Presence of God." Ezekiel 37:28 says: "And the heathen shall know that I the Lord do sanctify Israel, when my sanctuary shall be in the midst of them for evermore." There will be "the fullness of the Spirit." Joel 2:28a says: "And it shall come to pass afterward, that I will pour out my spirit upon all flesh." And there will be "the perpetuity of the millennial state." Amos 9:15 says: "And I will plant them upon their land, and they shall no more be pulled up out of their land which I have given them, saith the Lord thy God."

The Government

Let us now look at the government in the millennium. It will be administered by the King (Jesus Christ). It will be a theocracy. The power is in Christ, the King. But the living people are not machines. They have their will, which they exercise at the end of the reign; whether to follow Christ or the devil. Such a Kingdom was to be at the beginning in Eden. God was to rule and man dressing the garden. Man failed. God restores such a Kingdom as another opportunity for man to be obedient to God. Such is Love's final solution. Christ is in David's line and possesses the legal right to the throne. According to Matthew 19:28, authority over the twelve tribes of Israel will be vested in the hands of the twelve apostles. There will be lesser authorities, according to Luke 19:12-28. Some will be over ten cities, others over five cities and judges will be raised up. Isaiah 1:26 says: "And I will restore thy judges as at the first." It will be a universal reign, from verses already quoted. Israel is restored (Amos 9:14-15) in conversion of Israel as a nation (Rom. 11:26-27). Jerusalem is the center of worship. Palestine will be a fertile plain and productive. Isaiah 62:9 says: "But they that have gathered it shall eat it, and praise the Lord; and they that have brought it together shall drink it in the courts of my holiness."

Worship

Regarding the worship in the millennium, adoration will be given the Lord Jesus Christ (Isa. 66:23). There will be temple worship (Ezek. 41:1).

There will be an inner court. Ezek. 40:28 says, "And he brought me to the inner court by the south gate." There will be eight tables for sacrifices. Ezek. 40:41 says: "Four tables were on this side, and four tables on that side, by the side of the gate; eight tables, whereupon they slew their sacrifices." And there will be an altar where sacrifices are offered (Ezek. 40:47). The purpose of the temple is manifold:

1. To demonstrate God's holiness.
2. A dwelling place for divine glory. Ezekiel 43:5 says: "So the spirit took me up, and brought me into the inner court; and, behold, the glory of the Lord filled the house."
3. To perpetuate the memorial of sacrifice.
4. To provide the Centre for the divine government.
5. To provide victory over the Curse. Ezekiel 47:12 says: "And by the river upon the bank thereof, on this side and on that side, shall grow all trees for meat, whose leaf shall not fade, neither shall the fruit thereof be consumed: it shall bring forth new fruit according to his months, because their waters they issued out of the sanctuary; and the fruit thereof shall be for meat, and the leaf thereof for medicine."

Sacrifices

The sacrifices in the millennium are not for expiation or for salvation from sin. They will be memorial in character, a memorial of Christ's death. Hebrews 10:4-7 says, "For it is not possible that the blood of bulls and of goats should take away sins. Wherefore when he cometh into the world, he saith, Sacrifice and offering thou wouldst not, but a body hast thou prepared me: In burnt offerings and sacrifices for sin thou hast had no pleasure. Then said I, lo, I come (in the volume of the book it is written of me) to do thy will, O God." It is proof that the Church will not go through the millennium as an earth people – they reign with Christ. Let us also say that Ezekiel's temple is not Mosaic, but a new order for Israel in the millennium. This new covenant is also for those born in the millennium who need salvation. And this salvation will be based on the value of the death of Christ and will be by faith. Hebrews 11:6 says: "But without faith it is impossible to please him: for he that cometh to God must believe that he is, and that he is a rewarder of them that diligently seek him." Even as Abraham was justified by faith. Romans 4:3 says: "For what saith the Scripture? Abraham believed God, and it was counted unto him for righteousness." It is a remembrance of the work of Christ on which salvation rests.

A Difference

We must also recognize the relation between living and resurrected saints in the millennium. There has been confusion in Evangelical circles about the resurrected and translated saints of the church age; the resurrected saints of the Old Testament; and the living saints from among both Jews and Gentiles going without dying into the millennial age. We need to see their relation to the

King; their relation to the earth; and their relationship to each other.

1. It must be recognized that the Church shall reign with Christ.

2. The Old Testament saints are to be resurrected and rewarded in that age.

3. The saved Jews, found to be righteous at the judgment of Israel, together with the saved Gentiles, who are declared righteous at the judgment on the Gentiles at the time of the second Advent, are to be subjects of the King in the millennium (Matt. 25:31-46).

The national promises to Israel will be fulfilled on the earth in the millennium.

Why a 1000 Year Reign?

Let us then look at the Object of the thousand year reign:

1. Looked at from God the Father's side:

   a. It will be the public earthly honouring of His Son.

   b. It will be the carrying out of God's promises to His Son.

   c. It is the final divine trial of sinful man on earth.

   d. It is God's answer to the prayer of His saints "Thy Kingdom Come."

2. Looked at from Christ's side:

   a. He receives the Kingdom of this world.

   b. He gives the inheritance to the meek of the earth (Matt. 5).

   c. He shares His honours with the saints.

3. Looked at from the saints' side:

   a. The millennium brings the three classes of saints into a state of blessedness together with earthly Israel.

4. It will be a thousand years under the iron rod rule and yet there will be peace. And all the nations will go up every year to worship the King and keep the feast of tabernacles.

5. The creation shall be freed from the curse.

The Occupants

The occupants of the *heavenly Jerusalem* are given in Hebrews 11:13-16 and Hebrews 11:39-40: "And these all, having obtained a good report through faith, received not the promise: God having provided some better thing for us, that they without us should not be made perfect." They are the unfallen angels (Rev. 21:12); the resurrected and translated saints of the church-age, and all the resurrected Old Testament and Tribulation saints. It must be noted that this *heavenly* Jerusalem will not be the sphere of the living saved, who go into the millennium, for they will look to the rebuilt earthly Jerusalem as their capital city. Put it is rather the dwelling place of the resurrected saints, during the millennium. But all saints, living and resurrected, will serve one King.

The First Resurrection

The first resurrection applies to all individuals, of whatever age, who are raised to eternal life. But the resurrection takes place at different times in reference to different groups (Rev. 20:6). These are those having gone through tribulation and cannot apply only to church saints.

Hebrews 11:34-40 states: "And these all, having obtained a good report through faith, received not the promise: God having provided some better thing for us, that they without us should not be made perfect." This would indicate that the Old Testament saints cannot be made perfect until the body of Christ has been perfected. Thus, different stages of one resurrection. The new Jerusalem is God's dwelling even for eternity (Rev. 21:1-2). No other eternal habitation is seen. It has the glory of God in it (Rev. 21:11,23; 22:5). It has the throne of God in it (Rev. 22:3). And "they shall see His face." It is from this heavenly city that David's greater Son (according to the flesh) exerts His messianic rule.

Concerning the Second Advent

Four views of the Second Advent are mentioned for us by various commentators:

1. The non-literal or spiritualized view. It denies that there will be a literal, bodily, personal return of Christ to the earth. This view sees the second advent as the destruction of Jerusalem or the Day of Pentecost or the conversion of a person or any crisis in history. Some see the millennium as a time of darkness upon earth.

2. The postmillennial view. It believes that the whole world will be Christianized to the gospel before Christ's return.

3. The amillennial view. It believes that there will be no literal millennium on the earth following

the second advent. The Church fulfills the inter-advent period spiritually. Satan is considered bound with the first coming of Christ. Some believe we enter the millennium upon conversion.

4. The premillennial view. It holds that Christ will return to earth, bodily, before the millennial age begins in order to establish a Kingdom and reign over it for one thousand years. This Kingdom is earthly and visible. Matthew 25:31-34 reads: "When the Son of Man shall come in his glory, and all the holy angels with him, then shall he sit upon the throne of his glory: And before him shall be gathered all nations: and he shall separate them one from another, as a shepherd divideth his sheep from the goats: and he shall set the sheep on his right hand, but the goats on the left. Then shall the King say unto them on his right hand, Come, ye blessed of my Father, inherit the kingdom prepared for you from the foundation of the world."

Satan Loosed

At the end of the thousand years, Satan will be loosed. He will deceive the nations to go against the camp of the saints and the beloved city (Jerusalem) and they are "destroyed" by fire. The word "destroy" appears also in Matthew 10:28 where Jesus admonishes people not to be afraid of those who are able to kill the body but cannot kill the soul: rather to fear Him who is able to "destroy" both soul and body in "gehenna," (hell or lake of fire). The word "destroy" does not mean extinction but rather "to put out of the way, or "death" or "separation." The same word is used in Matthew 27:20 where the chief priests and the elders persuaded the crowd to ask for Barabbas to be freed and Jesus to be "destroyed." Jesus could not be extinguished (destroyed). The word "*apollumi*" (destroy) means death, separation or punish.

Failure

We see, therefore, that the kingdom age also ends in failure where people are tested as they choose which side they will support, the Lord's side or Satan's side. People were tested under "Innocence, Conscience, Self-government, Headship of the Family, Law and Grace and lastly under Christ or the influence of the Holy Spirit. And they proved themselves incurably bad and now comes the doom or judgment. Satan is cast into the Lake of fire (vs. 10), where the Beast and the False Prophet "*are*." Not "were." After one thousand years they are not consumed.

Judgments

And now we must note the various judgments in Scripture.

1. The judgment on sin. Since the fall of man into sin, there is in man the "bent or tendency" toward sin. The "will" of man is the reason for sinning and in the habit of sinning the bent or driving force grows stronger and becomes character. The first Adam wanted to taste, the second Adam chose not to. Jesus, therefore, died on the cross to save the sinner and change his character and make him a new-born child of

God. The sinner can, through Christ, escape from sin and judgment of hell.

2. The judgment upon the House of God. Luke 19:10 says: "For the Son of man is come to seek and to save that which was lost." The believer, too, needs to be warned of waywardness and its consequences. His judgment includes chastisement for fruitlessness. 1 Peter 4:17 says: "For the time is come that judgment must begin at the house of God: and if it first begin at us, what shall the end be of them that obey not the gospel of God?"

3. The judgment upon the believer's works. 2 Corinthians 5:10 says: "For we must all appear before the judgment seat of Christ; that everyone may receive the things done in his body, according to that he has done, whether it be good or bad." It is carried out at the judgment seat of Christ. Paul, in 1 Thessalonians 4, makes mention that this meeting is in the air. It is for the dead and living in Christ. They are examined *not* if they are believers, but, rather, to examine their works. The Greek word "*Bema*" represents not so much a judgment seat, but a platform from which rewards were given. Some will suffer loss and others gain. The gain is considered under the crowns that are presented.

4. The judgment upon the nations (Matt. 25:31-46). Verses 31-32 say: "When the Son of man shall come in his glory, and all the holy angels with him, then shall he sit upon the throne of his glory: And before him shall be

gathered all nations: and he shall separate them one from another, as a shepherd divideth his sheep from the goats." The Holy Spirit applied the word to all nations as a warning of a coming judgment. This is not like the judgment of Revelation 20. There is no mention here of resurrection. They are live nations and the judgment is upon earth and no books are opened. The Jewish nation is not counted among the nations. Numbers 23:9 says: "For from the top of the rocks I see him, and from the hills I behold him: lo, the people shall dwell alone, and shall not be reckoned among the nations." Nor is the Church mentioned. It is a judgment of nations and not of an individual. And the good nations will enter the millennium.

5. The Jewish Nation. The Jewish nation, too, will be judged as a nation. Romans 11:25-26a says: "For I would not, brethren, that ye should be ignorant of this mystery, lest ye should be wise in your own conceits: that blindness in part is happened to Israel, until the fullness of the Gentiles be come in. And so shall *all* Israel be saved." They rejected Jesus, but will accept Him and mourn for their wilfulness. Hosea 3:4-5 says, "For the children of Israel shall abide many days without a king, and without a prince, and without a sacrifice, and without an image, and without an ephod, and without teraphim: Afterward shall the children of Israel return, and seek the Lord their God, and David their king; and shall fear the Lord and his goodness in the latter days."

6. Satan will be judged and with him evil spirits and fallen angels. Revelation 20:10 and 15 say: "And the devil that deceived them was cast into the lake of fire and brimstone, where the beast and the false prophet *are*, and shall be tormented day and night for ever and ever. And whosoever was not found written in the book of life was cast into the lake of fire." The devil is not almighty, but God is. The devil is the prince of the air. He tries to get men to deny God. He offers the world systems to men as he did to Jesus.

White Throne Judgment

7. Then, lastly, there is the Great White Throne Judgment. It will take place at the end of the thousand year reign of Christ. He (Satan) shall be loosed and shall gather the nations against Christ and then shall be judged by Christ. This last judgment deals with the resurrection of the wicked whose names are not in the book of life. They are judged according to their works. Revelation 20:12 says: "And I saw the dead, small and great, stand before God; and the books were opened: and another book was opened, which is the book of life; and the dead were judged out of those things which were written in the books, according to their works." Revelation 20:15 says: "And whosoever was not found written in the book of life was cast into the lake of fire." It shows their reward. The Church is not in this judgment, nor is Israel. Both of these were judged – the Church at Calvary and Israel during the tribulation. This White Throne judgment is a judgment of the "dead"

and is called the "second resurrection." The difference of this judgment and that of Matthew 25:31-46 is this:

1. That of Matthew is on earth. This of Revelation 20 is from heaven.

2. That of Matthew is of living nations. This of Revelation 20 is of the dead resurrected.

3. That of Matthew is for the nations' treatment of Christ's brethren, Jews. This of Revelation 20 is for works.

4. There are no books opened in Matthew 25, but in Revelation 20 books are opened.

5. In Matthew no book of life is opened.

6. In Matthew judgment was before the millennium. In Revelation 20 it is after the thousand years.

Death and Hell

Death and hell are here personified (vs. 14). Death holds those bodies in the grave or sea. Hell holds the souls. Death and hell are cast into the lake of fire and this shows that they do not exist in eternity (heaven-nor on the new earth). The book of life is there to manifest their name being absent and the other books are to show their works. Books are unnecessary for God, but are mentioned for man to understand. Verse eleven shows the passing of heaven and earth. No place was found for them. This is not rejuvenation but a new creation. The devil had his day on earth and also had access to heaven as we note in the book of Job. Job 1:6 says: "Now there was a day when the sons of God came to present themselves before the Lord, and Satan came also among them." The devil is also the accuser of the brethren. Revelation 12:10b says: "For the accuser of our brethren is cast down, which accused them before our God day and night." Because of impurity found in the presence of the devil, the present earth and heaven shall pass away and there shall be a new earth and a new heaven. The earth and heaven fled away and no place was found for them (Rev. 20:11).

Resurrection Questions

Concerning verse thirteen of Revelation 20, we need to give some attention to the resurrection question. And we may ask:

What is involved in the resurrection? Some claim that there is no resurrection of the body, like the belief of the Sadducees. Others claim that only a spirit arises. Still others feel that only the soul arises. The Bible maintains that there is a resurrection of the body. The Greek word for resurrection is "*anastasis*" meaning "a raising up, rising." The Old Testament states in Daniel 12:2, "And many of them that sleep in the dust of the earth shall awake, some to everlasting life, and some to shame and everlasting contempt." And Isaiah 26:19a says: "Thy dead men shall live, together with my dead body shall they arise." Paul, in Romans 8:23b, says: "Even we ourselves groan within ourselves, waiting for the adoption, to wit, the redemption of our body." The resurrection is the most important fact of the gospel. Paul said, "If Christ be not raised, ye are yet in your sins."

First Fruit

The resurrection of Christ is described as the "first-fruits" (plural). During harvest the Hebrews would walk through the fields of standing grain and gather a handful of wheat heads and bind them in a sheaf. The priest would wave it before the Lord as an offering. This was done before the harvest proper was gathered. The first-fruits are therefore a preface to the words, "afterward they that are Christ's at his coming." The priest was to do this on the morrow after the Sabbath (Lev. 23:11). It was on the first day of the week. It prophesied of Christ's resurrection and of His becoming the first-fruits of them that slept. It was a sample of the entire crop. God will not disappoint nature and Satan will not have the last word. All the devil's works must be destroyed (1 John 3:8) and the Lord will have the victory when these corruptible bodies are raised from the grave as spiritual *bodies*. Here, then, are some reasons why we believe in the resurrection of the body:

Resurrection of the Body

1. God has honoured the body. It has become the temple of the Holy Spirit. The hope of the believer is not deliverance from the body, but its redemption.

2. Man cannot be a perfect being apart from the body. He consists of body, soul and spirit (1 Thess. 5:23).

3. The term "resurrection" denotes the raising of that which is placed in the earth (grave).

Michael and Satan strove over the body of Moses (Jude 9) but Moses' body was not given to Satan because it was useful to Moses later. It will be raised a "spiritual body" (1 Cor. 15:44). The word for body in this Scripture is "soma." It refers to the material body (translated into a spiritual body). 1 John 3:2 says: "Beloved, now are we the sons of God, and it doth not yet appear what we shall be: but we know that, when he shall appear, we shall be *like him*; for we shall see him *as he is*."

The Resurrection Order

The Word of God makes the claim that all shall be raised, but not at the same time. All shall be judged, but not at the same time. That is why we have such terms in the Bible as Heaven and hell – Hades, Gehenna, Lake of fire, Tartarus, Abyss and Pit. There is a resurrection of the righteous dead and a resurrection of the wicked dead. The one group to eternal life, the other to eternal damnation with one thousand year interval. The righteous are resurrected *not* because they are righteous in themselves, but they are so because of what Jesus did for them. Paul gives the order: "But every man in his own order: Christ the first-fruits: afterward they that are Christ's at his coming (Parousia) (presence) – then cometh the end" (1 Cor. 15:23-24).

Now, the word "first-fruits" is in the plural tense and would refer to the occurrence of the open graves after His resurrection and the bodies of the saints coming out of them and appearing to some people in the city (Matt. 27:52-53). The question arises as to what happened to them? And it can find an answer in Paul's statement in Ephesians 4:8: "Wherefore he saith, when he ascended up on high, he led captivity captive, and gave gifts unto men." These can very well be the first-fruits and along with them Jesus emptied the one compartment in hell (known as Abraham's bosom). These latter, however, must wait for the resurrected glorified body (1 Thess. 4). In this portion of Scripture, the dead in Christ shall rise first; then we which are alive and remain, shall be caught up together with them in the clouds, to meet the Lord in the air and so shall we ever be with the Lord. So it would follow that our natural bodies will be changed and become spiritual bodies like that of our Lord Jesus Christ. To this group, later will be added the tribulation saints and Old Testament saints. The others, outside of Christ, must be partakers of the great white throne judgment. Paul refers to this in 1 Corinthians 15:22 when he says, "For as in Adam all die, even so in Christ shall all be made alive" (not saved but alive). One might say that the first resurrection would seem to be one event in different stages. But no one is forgotten. Even the bones in the valley are not forgotten as Ezekiel 37:1-10 says. They came back to life. God is able to do the impossible with man.

The resurrection of Christ also supplements the creation of man. It reveals the foreknowledge of God. Man consists of body, soul and spirit. These parts are essential for world-consciousness, self-consciousness and God-consciousness. If one part is missing, then man is obviously not a human being. In this respect man is unlike the angels – they have no human body. They can appear as such, but it is not genuinely human. For this reason Christ came into the flesh. He was truly human and truly divine. Man also differs from the animals. No animal was like Adam in nature and reasoning ability. When God breathed into man the breath of life, man became a trinity similar to the trinity of God.

The Body

But the resurrection speaks only of the body. The soul and spirit are not subject to death and need no resurrection action. The body dies and decays, but is promised a resurrection; the redemption of the body (Rom. 8:23). Christ's body (flesh and bone; *not* flesh and blood) was raised gloriously. Such is the promise for the saints as well (1 John 3:2). This is not transfiguration but resurrection glory.

When the Sadducees asked Jesus about the resurrection, He answered: "God said: I am the God of Abraham, of Isaac and of Jacob... God is not the God of the dead but of the living." Note here, the words "I am" *not* "I was." These were dead long ago, but were living in God's presence, only awaiting the redemption of the body, to be united with the soul and spirit.

Physical Resurrection

There are many who deny a physical resurrection. They believe in a spiritual resurrection (of soul or spirit). Paul, in writing to the Philippians (3:21) says: "Who shall change our *vile body* that it may be fashioned like unto His glorious body." And His glorious body consisted of flesh and bone glorified. The blood was spilled, for flesh and blood cannot inherit the Kingdom of God. But flesh and bone glorified can and Jesus maintained that He had such. In Luke 24:39 He says: "Behold my hands and my feet, that it is I myself: handle me, and see; for a spirit hath not flesh and bones, as ye see me have." If Christ's body had not risen and had decayed, He would be a spirit and if a spirit, then He is not a glorified man and cannot be a Mediator. He is not then the "Son of man" as seen by John and there could not be salvation through Him, for that comes not by way of angels or spirits, but by the shedding of blood (Heb. 2). His, however, is the resurrected body glorified. An apt illustration of this is the calling into life the dry bones in Ezekiel 37:4-5: "Again he said unto me, prophesy upon these bones, and say unto them, O ye dry bones, hear the word of the Lord. Thus saith the Lord God unto these bones. Behold I will cause breath to enter into you, and ye shall live."

Justification

The significance of the resurrection is essential for justification of the act of atonement made on the cross of Calvary. Now, then, what does the resurrection signify?

1. It is a revelation of the power of God. In the resurrection He moves upon the threshold of the enemy and overcomes death and hell and places the privilege at our disposal. We, too, may overcome.

2. The resurrection is proof that Jesus Christ is the Son of God. Hebrews 10:5 says: "a *body* hast thou prepared me." He became, therefore, the firstborn of those who should be fashioned like unto His body.

3. The resurrection reveals that He is more than a Saviour. He is Lord. That, on our part, involves total commitment to Him. He needs to be on the throne of our hearts.

4. He is our Righteousness. We cannot approach God in our own righteousness. We are accounted righteous only through Christ.

5. The resurrection is the seal and sign that Jesus is the judge of all (2 Cor. 5:10). And it is the assurance that all shall rise.

6. The resurrection reveals Christ to be King of kings and Lord of lords. He shall rule all nations. Revelation 20:6 says: "Blessed and holy is he that hath part in the first resurrection; on such the second death hath no power, but they shall be priests of God and of Christ, and shall reign with him a thousand years."

No Soul Sleep

Revelation 20:15 says: "And whosoever was not found written in the book of life was cast into the lake of fire." There is no room here for soul sleeping, for an intermediate state, for a second chance, or for annihilation of the wicked (Dan. 12:2; John 5:28-29).

New Heaven and Earth

Events

Before we go into details of this chapter, we need to enumerate a few facts in regard to certain events. We have here:

1. The ages to come have a new heaven and a new earth. When we talk about animals in heaven, we tend to forget the new earth on which we shall, no doubt, behold surprises of that which God has in store for us.

2. The new Jerusalem. It would seem to be the capital of the universe. Paul says to the Galatians (4:26) that the Jerusalem on earth answers to Agar as Mount Sinai; but "Jerusalem, which is above, is free, which is the mother of us all."

3. The new and eternal people and conditions (vs. 4-7). They are redeemed and justified by their works. It is the righteous position we have *after* our works have been judged.

4. The second death which is a separation of the wicked from God and Christ (vs. 8).

5. The true Bride of Christ and her identity. Babylon, the false pretending church has been destroyed and is fallen and separated to the unbelievers doom.

6. The outward appearance of Jerusalem (vs. 11). It is holy.

7. The walls, twelve gates which bear the names of the twelve tribes of Israel and twelve foundations which bear the names of the twelve apostles of the Church (vs. 12-15).

8. The measurements (vs. 16-17).

9. The materials (vs. 18-21).

10. The temple (vs. 22).

11. The Light (vs. 23).

12. The traffic in the New Jerusalem (vs. 24-27).

The New Heaven and New Earth

Here in this chapter and chapter twenty-two we have the seven *new* things. There is a new heaven and a new earth and no more sea. This is not a cleansing, as some believe, but, as Revelation 20:11 says, "And there was found *no* place for them." And verse five says: "Behold, I make all things new." Isaiah 65:17 says, "For, behold, I create new heavens and a new earth; and the former shall not be remembered, nor come into mind." Also read Isaiah 66:22 and 2 Peter 3:13 which say: "Nevertheless we, according to his promise, look for new heavens and a new earth, wherein dwelleth righteousness." The old physical world is gone in this vision. It is not a picture of renovation of this earth, but of the disappearance of this earth and sky. And the new earth has a new metropolis. A New Jerusalem where our real citizenship is. For besides a new heaven and a new earth, there will be a new people, a new fellowship as in Eden before the Fall. Verse eight says that all the wicked will be in the lake of fire. Verse four is a comfort to every believer. There will be no more tears, for that which causes tears, will be removed. Death is no more, nor mourning which is associated with death and crying. And pain is gone. There is peace and bliss. This is Love's Final Solution.

Alpha and Omega

Verse three shows God's intention, from the beginning, to have fellowship with man and verse six is a personal testimony. It describes God (God-head) as "*Alpha.*" This is the first letter of the Greek alphabet and carries the meaning of the "creative God." "*Omega*" is the last letter of the Greek alphabet and designates God as the "eternal God," and as such He is able to give to the over-comer the water of life. It shows a personal rela-tionship in which life radiates from God to a dependent follower. It is a close personal connec-tion and relationship. Verse seven shows and car-ries that intimate relationship still farther, as a father to a son. An obedient son will want to be an overcomer in order to be in the will of his father and, holding his father's hand, he will not stray. But the wrongdoer (vs. 8), will face separation through lack of close relationship and fellowship. The first death is that of the body; the second death of the wicked is eternal death. It is not anni-hilation, as is shown by the antichrist and false prophet still being in the lake of fire when, after a thousand years, the devil joins them. In that place are the fearful (cowardly), the unbelieving (untrustworthy), the abominable (who pollute) (who defile), the murderers, the fornicators, the idolaters (connected with magic) and all liars.

The New Jerusalem

Verse nine shows the Bride as if the marriage is not yet a reality. The city is shown as the Lamb's wife. It is the new Jerusalem. God's very presence is in the Holy City. Christ is the light of the world (John 8:12) and so are Christians (Matt. 5:14). And we have seven names of the city of God:

1. The holy city (vs. 2).
2. The new Jerusalem (vs. 2).
3. The tabernacle of God (vs. 3).
4. The Bride, the Lamb's wife (vs. 9).
5. The holy Jerusalem (vs. 10).
6. The heavenly Jerusalem (Heb. 12:22).
7. The Father's House (John 14:2).

Blessings

Then let us look at the blessings for man in the new earth:

1. God will be dwelling among the inhabitants (vs. 3).
2. God will be their God. None other is anticipated (vs. 3,7).
3. God shall wipe away all tears (vs. 4).
4. There shall be no more death (vs. 4).

5. There shall be no more sorrow; pain (vs. 4).

6. All things are made new (vs. 5).

7. There shall be plenty of water of life (vs. 4). It will be an everflowing fountain.

8. The overcomers shall inherit all things (vs. 7). They shall be joint heirs with Christ (Rom. 8:17).

9. There shall be eternal sonship (vs. 7).

10. There shall be no more curse (22:3).

11. There will be freedom from ungodly neighbours (vs. 8).

The new city comes down out of heaven to earth. It is fifteen hundred miles square. It could be a cube or a pyramid. The inhabitants are the angels, the Church, tribulation saints and saints of Israel (vs. 12-14). It is a city with no temple. God and the Lamb are the temple. The new light is the glory of God and the Lamb. No one should forget the sacrifice of Jesus. Into this city the saved nations (who are worthy) shall bring their glory. Let us look at the life in the eternal city:

Life in the City

1. It is a life of fellowship with God, the Lamb and the Holy Spirit. 1 John 3:2 says: "Beloved, now are we the sons of God, and it doth not yet appear what we shall be: but we know that, when he shall appear, we shall be like him; for we shall see him as he is."

2. It is a life of rest with no evil disturbance. Revelation 14:13 says: "And I heard a voice from

heaven saying unto me, Write, Blessed are the dead which die in the Lord from henceforth: Yea, saith the Spirit, that they may rest from their labours; and their works do follow them."

3. It is a life of full knowledge. 1 Corinthians 13:12b says: "Now I know in part; but then shall I know even as also I am known." Memory is cleansed and remains and is increased. In Luke 16:19-31, Abraham said to the rich man, "Son, remember...."

4. It is a life of holiness (Rev. 21:27).

5. It is a life of joy (Rev. 21:4).

6. It is a life of service. Revelation 22:3 says: "And there shall be no more curse: but the throne of God and of the Lamb shall be in it; and his servants shall serve him." It will be "*doulos*" (Greek) service – with total commitment.

7. It will be a life of abundance. Revelation 21:6b says: "I will give unto him that is athirst of the fountain of the water of life freely." This shows the capability of the resurrected and glorified Christ.

8. It is a life of glory. 2 Corinthians 4:17 says: "For our light affliction, which is but for a moment, worketh for us a far more exceeding and eternal weight of glory."

9. It is a life of worship. Revelation 19:1 says: "And after these things I heard a great voice of much people in heaven, saying, Alleluia; Salvation, and glory, and honour, and power, unto the Lord our God." It shall be without distraction.

Realizing that kind of a life in Christ, we need to cry out with the angels: "Worthy is the Lamb that was slain to receive power, and riches, and wisdom, and strength, and honour, and glory, and blessing" (Rev. 5:12).

Mansions

The dwellers of the new Jerusalem, "shall reign unto the ages of the ages." (Greek of Rev. 22:5). It would seem to be the place of which the Lord spoke in John 14:2-3. "In my Father's house are many mansions: if it were not so, I would have told you. I go to prepare a place for you. And if I go and prepare a place for you, I will come again, and receive you unto myself; that where I am, there ye may be also." Shelter speaks of safety from storms and assures comfort and warmth. It is Love's Final Solution. The light of the city shall lighten the earth so that the nations shall walk in it and bring their glory unto it (Rev. 21:24). There may, also, be two descents of the city in chapter 21 – one at the beginning of the millennium and the other at the commencement of the eternal state. It is of utmost concern that our names are written in the Lamb's book of life.

Overview

Let us first look at this chapter and consider an overview. We have here, in the interior of the city:

1. The rivers, streets and fruit of the New Jerusalem (vs. 1-2).

2. The rulers of the New Jerusalem (vs. 3-5).

3. The confirmation of the Book (vs. 6). "And he said unto me, These sayings are faithful and true."

4. The blessings for keeping the Truths of the book (vs. 7). "Blessed is he that keepeth the sayings of the prophecy of this book."

5. A common mistake in worship (vs. 8-9). "And when I had heard and seen, I fell down to worship before the feet of the angel which showed me these things. Then saith he unto me. See thou do it not: for I am thy fellowservant, and of thy brethren the prophets, and of them which keep the sayings of this book: worship God."

6. The command not to seal the book (vs. 10).

"And he saith unto me, seal not the sayings of the prophecy of this book: for the time is at hand."

7. The eternal state of men to be as they are when they die (vs. 11). "He that is unjust, let him be unjust still: and he which is filthy, let him be filthy still: and he that is righteous, let him be righteous still: and he that is holy, let him be holy still."

8. Christ's coming predicted (vs. 12-13). "Behold I come quickly: and my reward is with me, to give every man according as his work shall be. I am Alpha and Omega, the beginning and the end, the first and the last."

9. The last blessing for those who keep the truths of the book (vs. 14).

10. The last warnings against sinning and eternal punishment (vs. 15).

11. Authenticity of the book affirmed (vs. 16). "I Jesus have sent my angel to testify unto you these things in the churches. I am the root and the offspring of David, and the bright and morning star."

12. An invitation to all men to be saved (vs. 17). "And the Spirit and the bride say, Come. And let him that heareth say, Come. And let him that is athirst come. And whosoever will, let him take the water of life freely."

13. A warning to all men (vs. 18-19). Not to add, nor to take away any part of the book and the things that are written therein.

14. Conclusion and Benediction (vs. 20-21). "Even so, come Lord Jesus."

A New River and Tree of Life

Now let us go back and look at the chapter a little more closely. Another new thing, among others, is the new river. It is not polluted. It is a river of life because of its life-giving qualities. It has its source in the throne of God and of the Lamb. Life flows only from God through Christ. Christ is pictured as sharing the Father's throne. There is also a new tree of life and what a tree it is. It bears twelve kinds of fruit. It would seem a different kind each month and it is for the overcomers. Revelation 2:7 says: "To him that overcometh will I give to eat of the tree of life, which is in the midst of the paradise of God." The leaves shall be for the healing of the nations. It is to show their dependence on God. It is for those nations that occupy the new earth. Just as Adam would have remained in health if he had eaten of the Tree of Life in the garden of Eden. Genesis 3:22 says: "And the Lord God said, behold, the man is become as one of us, to know good and evil: and now, lest he put forth his hand, and take also of the tree of life, and eat, and live forever; Therefore the Lord God sent him forth from the garden of Eden."

The Throne

Then we are made aware of the new Throne. Verses three and four say: "And there shall be no more curse: but the throne of God and of the Lamb shall be in it; and his servants shall serve him: And they shall see his face...." This vision of God was withheld from Moses (Exod. 33:20), but promised by Jesus to the pure in heart (Matt. 5:8). There is no Temple for the object of worship is present. We shall see Him and when we see, when our eyes are opened, we shall see that we are like Him in our translated, spiritual bodies. And we shall be able to praise our Lord for all He has done for us.

God in Christ

Verses six and seven show that Christ is speaking and He has been the Inspirer of the prophets. The Greek has it as "God of the spirits of the prophets." Here are revealed and gathered together all the revelations of God in the Old Testament. The Lord God is the Adonai, Elohim, Jehovah, The Almighty. Jesus declares Himself all of these in verses thirteen and sixteen. He is the One of the Old Testament and the New Testament. He is the One of the Covenants (A testament or agreement). There are eight of them. We repeat:

Covenants

1. *The Edenic.* Genesis 2:15 says: "And the Lord God took the man, and put him into the garden of Eden to dress it and keep it."

2. *The Adamic.* Genesis 3:15 says: "And I will put enmity between thee and the woman, and between thy seed and her seed; it shall bruise thy head, and thou shalt bruise his heel."

3. *The Noahic.* Genesis 9:1 says: "And God blessed Noah and his sons, and said unto them, Be fruitful, and multiply, and replenish the earth."

4. *The Abrahamic.* Genesis 15:18 says: "In the same day the Lord made a covenant with Abram, saying, Unto thy seed have I given this land, from the river of Egypt unto the great river, the river Euphrates."

5. *The Mosaic.* Exodus 19:5 says: "Now, therefore, if ye will obey my voice indeed, and keep my covenant, then ye shall be a peculiar treasure unto me above all people..".

6. *The Palestinian.* Deuteronomy 30:3 says: "That then the Lord thy God will turn thy captivity, and have compassion upon thee, and will return and gather thee from all the nations, whither the Lord thy God hath scattered thee."

7. *The Davidic.* 2 Samuel 7:16 says: "And thine house and thy kingdom shall be established for ever before thee: thy throne shall be established for ever."

8. *New.* Hebrews 8:8 says: "For finding fault with them, he saith, Behold, the days come, saith the Lord, when I will make a new covenant with the house of Israel and with the house of Judah."

Dispensations

Also He is the One of the Dispensations. This is a period of time during which man is tested in respect of obedience to some revelation of the will of God. The Greek for dispensation is stewardship. These dispensations of testing are:

1. *Innocency* (In Eden).

2. *Conscience.* Genesis 3:7 says: "And the eyes of them both were opened, and they knew that

they were naked; and they sewed fig leaves together, and made themselves aprons" (vs. 9). "And the Lord God called unto Adam, and said unto him, Where art thou? And he said, I heard thy voice in the garden, and I was afraid, because I was naked; and I hid myself."

3. *Human Government.* Genesis 8:20 says: "And Noah builded an altar unto the Lord; and took of every clean beast, and of every clean fowl, and offered burnt offerings on the altar."

4. *Promise.* Genesis 12:1 says: "Now the Lord has said unto Abram, Get thee out of thy country, and from thy kindred, and from thy father's house, unto a land that I will show thee."

5. *Law.* Exodus 19:8 says: "And all the people answered together, and said, all that the Lord hath spoken we will do. And Moses returned the words of the people unto the Lord."

6. *Grace.* John 1:17 says: "For the law was given by Moses, but grace and truth came by Jesus Christ."

7. *Kingdom.* Ephesians 1:10 says: "That in the dispensation of the fullness of times he might gather together in one all things in Christ, both which are in heaven, and which are on earth; even in Him."

8. Last of all, the *fullness of Times* – the gathering together in one all things in Christ.

Final Triumph

Then look at the blessing in verse seven. "Blessed is he that keepeth the sayings of the prophecy of this book." It is the prophecy of this book of Revelation. His coming is according to God's time, not ours. And His coming is a comforting picture of final triumph and bliss for the faithful. And it is for all to read and observe. John was so taken up with the sight of heavenly things that he was willing to worship anyone in that area. But the angel prevented such an act and revealed himself as a fellow servant of and with John and the prophets and of them that keep the sayings of this book. That reveals the importance of our interest in the revelation of God through Christ our Redeemer and Lord. The book is not sealed and all will be fulfilled in God's own time. And we are to remember the words of Peter that with God one day is as a thousand years. Verse eleven shows that the states of both the evil and the good are now fixed forever.

Exclusions

The residents have a right to the tree of life (vs. 14). We see, also, those who are excluded from the city (vs. 15). "For without are dogs, and sorcerers, and whoremongers, and murderers, and idolaters, and whosoever loveth and maketh a lie." The word "without" in the Greek is "outside" and carries the meaning "away from or separated." We are dealing here with Alpha ages (creative ages) and Omega ages (of the ages of the ages), all handed over to the Father so that God is all in all. The message is not just for the seven churches but for all the churches in the world then and now.

The Alpha and Omega

Much has been said about salvation, but very

little about the Saviour as the Alpha and Omega of verse thirteen. We know that Alpha is the first letter of the Greek alphabet and Omega the last. It is as if He is saying, "I am A and Z, I am the alphabet." The alphabet takes on meaning as He gives it meaning. Long ago Moses was grazing his sheep in a desert when he saw a fiery bush not being destroyed by fire, and as he came near there was a voice warning him to remove his shoes as he was standing on holy ground. The Lord spoke to Moses and asked him to lead His people out of Egypt. When Moses asked His name, He answered "I Am." Moses was to say to the Israelites, "I Am" has sent me. But who is this "I Am?" For some time "I Am" stood alone. Then it took on meaning. With the birth of Christ, we have the fulfillment of the "I Am." Jesus said, "I am the bread of life; I am the Light of the world; I am the Door; I am the good shepherd; I am the vine; I am the Way, the Truth, the Life; I am the resurrection"; until He comes to "I am Alpha and Omega." One might say, this is a revelation of the inexhaustibility of Christ. Innumerable books have been written displaying knowledge and wisdom. But all those books are done with twenty-six letters of the alphabet. What the alphabet is to these books, Christ, the ALPHABET, is to life of man. Who is capable to explain the mystery of His birth and crucifixion and resurrection and ascension? And only He can explain and fulfill the question that Nicodemus asked: "How can a man be born when he is old? Who can explain His wisdom and love?"

This is also a revelation of the Victory of Christ. "A" is the first letter in the alphabet and there is no letter after "Z." He is "before" time; He is "in" time and He is "forever" (after time). As Paul says to the Ephesian church: "Unto Him be glory in the Church by Christ Jesus throughout all ages, world without end. Amen" (Eph. 3:21). And this is a revelation of adaptability. The alphabet can be used wherever a tongue moves between lips and forms words. We can understand each other and communicate with each other and fellowship with each other with the letters of the alphabet. The lover or the poet or the musician can all make use of the alphabet. So Jesus desires to be available to all of us and by accepting Him as Saviour, He fills us and uses us as we use the alphabet. He is "the Alpha and Omega, the beginning and the end, the first and the last."

In verse sixteen Jesus calls Himself the "Morning Star." This star appears before the "Sun of Righteousness." *Grace* is still offered before judgment and the end of all things. The Sun of Righteousness is the revelation of Christ. Malachi 4:2 says: "But unto you that fear my name shall the Sun of righteousness arise with healing in his wings." So Christ reveals Love's final solution.

The Ascension

Between the resurrection and reappearance of Christ stands the ascension of Christ. It is not easy to follow Him as He passes out of sight. And yet He is as much alive today as ever. And John sees Him all glorious at the right hand of God, even as Stephen, the martyr who was stoned, saw the Lord "standing on the right hand of God." Jesus is also the man Christ Jesus just as Abraham, Moses and

Elijah. But Jesus in heaven is more complete than all of these, for He has already the resurrected glorified body. God allowed the bodies of Enoch and Elijah to pass, but Jesus in his own power passed into heaven. And when Jesus passed into heaven, it was the arrival of One as had never before been there. He is the Lamb of God but also the Son of man. No wonder the angels, who desired to look into Christ's coming to earth, now must have looked upon His glorified body, with wonder. They gazed with wonder upon that dear body, having been crucified for the salvation of mankind. He is now the Lamb that can loose the seals and open the book (6:1). Paul, in writing to Timothy says: "God gave us the Spirit of power and of love and of a sound mind" (2 Tim. 1:7). Christ practiced these and now in heaven "He is the King of glory," the Living One, "and I was dead, and behold, I am alive forevermore."

Why Death?

The mystery of life cannot be explained in a scientific way. It is said that the human body reconstructs itself once in every seven years. One wonders why this process cannot continue indefinitely? Why death? There is no answer except for revelation that gives the answer. Death is the penalty for sin; Christ has overcome death and given eternal life; life that has no ending. The ascension is proof of all of that. Mark 16:19 says: "So then after the Lord had spoken unto them, he was received up into heaven, and sat on the right hand of God." That is His exalted position. Of such exalted meaning consists the ascension. Let us look at that meaning:

271

The Ascension

1. The ascension is proof that He is the Son of God. We are reminded that we must look at, not so much His bodily absence, but His "spiritual presence." He has changed earthly limitations into life eternal, when He says: "Because I live, ye shall live also" (John 14:19). The ascension is the focal point of the salvation process. Christ's ascension reveals the acceptable righteousness which God required of His Son in obedience to the Father's will. 2 Corinthians 5:21 says: "For he hath made him to be sin for us, who knew no sin; that we might be made the righteousness of God in him." When John saw Christ (the Son of man) in Revelation 1:13-14, he saw Jesus' eyes as "a flame of fire." That shows resplendent righteousness acceptable to God.

The ascension also reveals Christ as High Priest who prepares the way of approach to God by man. Only through Christ can man come before God and find fellowship with his God. A fellowship that had been broken. The ascension also recognizes Christ as the Head of the Church. Ephesians 1:19-23 says: "And what is the exceeding greatness of his power to usward who believe, according to the working of his mighty power. Which he wrought in Christ when he raised him from the dead, and set him at his own right hand in the heavenly places. Far above all principality, and power, and might, and dominion, and every name that is named, not only in this world, but also in that which is to come: And hath put all things under his feet, and gave him to be the head over all things to the Church. Which is his body."

Mediation

The crowning value of the ascension is mediation. Christ is the Mediator between us and the Father. Romans 8:34 says: "Who is he that condemneth? It is Christ that died, yea rather, that is risen again, who is even at the right hand of God, who also maketh intercession for us."

Pentecost

There is also a relationship between the ascension and Pentecost. For Christ sent the Holy Spirit upon the disciples as the Gift of the Father to Him. John 14:26 says: "But the Comforter, which is the Holy Ghost, whom the Father will send in *my name*, he shall teach you all things." In this sense Jesus was able to say: "And, lo, I am with you alway, even unto the end of the world" (Greek: "and behold I am with you all the days until the completion of the age").

The aim of the ascension is the consummation of all things. "And he that sat upon the throne said: Behold, I make all things new" (Rev. 21:5). And Hebrews 10:12 says: "But this man, after he had offered one sacrifice for sins forever, sat down on the right hand of God; from henceforth expecting till his enemies be made his footstool."

Since, after His ascension, Jesus sent the Holy Spirit to abide in His own, therefore, the Spirit and the Bride say "Come" to Jesus. And everyone is to listen and hear the invitation in the acceptable time period. The invitation is open and freely given. And it is given by the Holy Spirit who has a close and intimate relationship with the Bride (Church). Therefore we need to consider also the third Person of the Trinity.

Pentecost Enlarged

At Pentecost the Holy Spirit descended like the sound of a mighty rushing wind. The one hundred and twenty people gathered in prayer, waiting for an answer to their prayers, did not question the miracle of the coming of that tremendous life-surge. A miracle took place. Something new breathed into their lives, and they were never quite the same again. And this happening the Spirit and the Bride are desirous of sharing with others who are thirsty and needy. For the Christian, the filling of the Holy Spirit, is life in the soul, the openheart-edness that says: "Come, Holy Spirit." All of us have been faced with some crisis we felt we could not conquer but did, and something out of nowhere possessed us, fired us, lifted us, calmed us, helped us, healed us, restored us, until we were not only ourselves but inspired by the Holy Spirit. We found what we could not do on our own, God helped us do. That is the force which creates new lives. The same power that created man out of dust, that created the living Church out of a small group of mourning disciples. No less divine than the miracle of birth is the miracle of rebirth by the Holy Spirit. That is the reason of the call of the Holy Spirit to the "whosoevers" that are athirst. His supreme work is to convince people and to convict them, to cleanse and renew them and make them over in the likeness of Christ. Therefore the fruit of the Spirit is: love, joy, peace, patience, kindness, goodness, faithfulness, gentleness and self-control. We do not make Christians of ourselves, we open our lives in faith to the cleansing, renewing breath of God and Christ, and the Spirit produces these graces within us. And people who live in a world of unrest and poverty and turmoil, fragmentation and frustration, need to learn of Christ and how the Spirit given by Christ can restore them to a people with admissibility to the New Jerusalem. 1 Corinthians 12:13 says: "For by one Spirit are we all baptized into one body." Which means that Christians belong to the fellowship of Christ. John speaks for the Church when he says, "Amen. Even so, come, Lord Jesus."

The Old and New Testaments

The Old Testament ended with a curse. Malachi 4:6 says: "And he shall turn the heart of the fathers to the children, and the heart of the children to their fathers, lest I come and smite the earth with a curse." The New Testament ends with the word "Grace." Revelation 22:21 says: "The grace of our Lord Jesus Christ be with you all." It denotes joy, delight, loveliness. Also good will, mercy and kindness upon the undeserving. And unmerited favour to those whom the love of God would save. This is Love's Final Solution.

Closing Message

And no one is to add or take away from the revelation that God in Christ has revealed to man. As God, in the beginning, commanded His people to be obedient, for He said in Deuteronomy 4:2, "Ye shall not add unto the word which I command you, neither shall ye diminish ought from it," so He gives us the warning through John. Verses eighteen and nineteen say: "For I testify unto every man that heareth the words of the prophecy of this book, if any man shall add unto these things, God shall add unto him the plagues that are written in this book. And if any man shall take away from the words of the book of this prophecy, God shall take away his part out of the book of life, and out of the holy city, and from the things which are written in this book." Let us heed this admonition and abide thereby and obtain eternal life in Jesus.

Let us close our dissertation on Revelation by quoting once more verses eighteen and nineteen from the Amplified Bible: "I (personally solemnly) warn every one who listens to the statements of the prophecy (the predictions and the consolations and admonitions pertaining to them) in this book: if anyone shall add anything to them, God will add and lay upon him the plagues – the afflictions and the calamities – that are recorded and described in this book.

And if any one cancels or takes away from the statements of the book of this prophecy – these predictions relating to Christ's Kingdom and its speedy triumph, together with the consolations and admonitions (warnings) pertaining to them – God will cancel and take away share in the tree of life and in the city of holiness (pure and hallowed) which are described and promised in this book." Psalm 119:89 says: "For ever, O Lord, thy word is settled in heaven."

Comparisons

By way of comparison, I have referred to various expositors and writers and commentaries.

Things to Come, by J. Dwight Pentecost.

Word Pictures of The New Testament, by Archibald Thomas Robertson.

The Scofield Bible, by C.I. Scofield.

Strong's Concordance

Thayer's Greek-English Lexicon of the New Testament.

The Book of Revelation, by C. Larkin.

The Two Babylons, by Hislop.

Swete